FERDINAND MARCOS

FERDINAND MARCOS

Gordy Slack

921
Mar

18110

CHELSEA HOUSE PUBLISHERS
NEW YORK
NEW HAVEN   PHILADELPHIA

Chelsea House Publishers

EDITOR-IN-CHIEF: Nancy Toff
EXECUTIVE EDITOR: Remmel T. Nunn
MANAGING EDITOR: Karyn Gullen Browne
COPY CHIEF: Juliann Barbato
PICTURE EDITOR: Adrian G. Allen
ART DIRECTOR: Giannella Garrett
MANUFACTURING MANAGER: Gerald Levine

World Leaders

SENIOR EDITOR: John W. Selfridge

Staff for FERDINAND MARCOS:

ASSISTANT EDITOR: Kathleen McDermott
DEPUTY COPY CHIEF: Ellen Scordato
EDITORIAL ASSISTANT: Sean Ginty
ASSOCIATE PICTURE EDITOR: Juliette Dickstein
PICTURE RESEARCHER: Elie Porter
DESIGNER: Jill Goldreyer
PRODUCTION COORDINATOR: Joseph Romano
COVER ILLUSTRATION: Peter Fiore

First Printing

1 3 5 7 9 8 6 4 2

Library of Congress Cataloging in Publication Data

Slack, Gordy.
Ferdinand Marcos.

(World leaders past & present)
Bibliography: p.
Includes index.
  Summary: Examines the life of the Philippine political leader whose
presidency was viewed by some as a dictatorship.

1. Marcos, Ferdinand E. (Ferdinand Edralin), 1917–   .
2. Philippines—Presidents—Biography—Juvenile literature.
[1. Marcos, Ferdinand E. (Ferdinand Edralin), 1917–   .
2. Philippines—Presidents] I. Title. II. Series.
DS686.6.M35S53   1988   959.9′046′0924 [B] [92]   87-32653

ISBN 1-55546-842-X

Contents

John Adams
John Quincy Adams
Konrad Adenauer
Alexander the Great
Salvador Allende
Marc Antony
Corazon Aquino
Yasir Arafat
King Arthur
Hafez al-Assad
Kemal Atatürk
Attila
Clement Attlee
Augustus Caesar
Menachem Begin
David Ben-Gurion
Otto von Bismarck
Léon Blum
Simon Bolívar
Cesare Borgia
Willy Brandt
Leonid Brezhnev
Julius Caesar
John Calvin
Jimmy Carter
Fidel Castro
Catherine the Great
Charlemagne
Chiang Kai-Shek
Winston Churchill
Georges Clemenceau
Cleopatra
Constantine the Great
Hernán Cortés
Oliver Cromwell
Georges-Jacques
    Danton
Jefferson Davis
Moshe Dayan
Charles de Gaulle
Eamon De Valera
Eugene Debs
Deng Xiaoping
Benjamin Disraeli
Alexander Dubček
François & Jean-Claude
    Duvalier
Dwight Eisenhower
Eleanor of Aquitaine
Elizabeth i
Faisal
Ferdinand & Isabella
Francisco Franco
Benjamin Franklin

Frederick the Great
Indira Gandhi
Mohandas Gandhi
Giuseppe Garibaldi
Amin & Bashir Gemayel
Genghis Khan
William Gladstone
Mikhail Gorbachev
Ulysses S. Grant
Ernesto "Che" Guevara
Tenzin Gyatso
Alexander Hamilton
Dag Hammarskjöld
Henry viii
Henry of Navarre
Paul von Hindenburg
Hirohito
Adolf Hitler
Ho Chi Minh
King Hussein
Ivan the Terrible
Andrew Jackson
James i
Wojciech Jaruzelski
Thomas Jefferson
Joan of Arc
Pope John xxiii
Pope John Paul ii
Lyndon Johnson
Benito Juárez
John Kennedy
Robert Kennedy
Jomo Kenyatta
Ayatollah Khomeini
Nikita Khrushchev
Kim Il Sung
Martin Luther King, Jr.
Henry Kissinger
Kublai Khan
Lafayette
Robert E. Lee
Vladimir Lenin
Abraham Lincoln
David Lloyd George
Louis xiv
Martin Luther
Judas Maccabeus
James Madison
Nelson & Winnie
    Mandela
Mao Zedong
Ferdinand Marcos
George Marshall

Mary, Queen of Scots
Tomáš Masaryk
Golda Meir
Klemens von Metternich
James Monroe
Hosni Mubarak
Robert Mugabe
Benito Mussolini
Napoléon Bonaparte
Gamal Abdel Nasser
Jawaharlal Nehru
Nero
Nicholas II
Richard Nixon
Kwame Nkrumah
Daniel Ortega
Mohammed Reza Pahlavi
Thomas Paine
Charles Stewart
    Parnell
Pericles
Juan Perón
Peter the Great
Pol Pot
Muammar el-Qaddafi
Ronald Reagan
Cardinal Richelieu
Maximilien Robespierre
Eleanor Roosevelt
Franklin Roosevelt
Theodore Roosevelt
Anwar Sadat
Haile Selassie
Prince Sihanouk
Jan Smuts
Joseph Stalin
Sukarno
Sun Yat-sen
Tamerlane
Mother Teresa
Margaret Thatcher
Josip Broz Tito
Toussaint L'Ouverture
Leon Trotsky
Pierre Trudeau
Harry Truman
Queen Victoria
Lech Walesa
George Washington
Chaim Weizmann
Woodrow Wilson
Xerxes
Emiliano Zapata
Zhou Enlai

CHELSEA HOUSE PUBLISHERS

ON LEADERSHIP

Arthur M. Schlesinger, jr.

LEADERSHIP, it may be said, is really what makes the world go round. Love no doubt smooths the passage; but love is a private transaction between consenting adults. Leadership is a public transaction with history. The idea of leadership affirms the capacity of individuals to move, inspire, and mobilize masses of people so that they act together in pursuit of an end. Sometimes leadership serves good purposes, sometimes bad; but whether the end is benign or evil, great leaders are those men and women who leave their personal stamp on history.

Now, the very concept of leadership implies the proposition that individuals can make a difference. This proposition has never been universally accepted. From classical times to the present day, eminent thinkers have regarded individuals as no more than the agents and pawns of larger forces, whether the gods and goddesses of the ancient world or, in the modern era, race, class, nation, the dialectic, the will of the people, the spirit of the times, history itself. Against such forces, the individual dwindles into insignificance.

So contends the thesis of historical determinism. Tolstoy's great novel *War and Peace* offers a famous statement of the case. Why, Tolstoy asked, did millions of men in the Napoleonic Wars, denying their human feelings and their common sense, move back and forth across Europe slaughtering their fellows? "The war," Tolstoy answered, "was bound to happen simply because it was bound to happen." All prior history predetermined it. As for leaders, they, Tolstoy said, "are but the labels that serve to give a name to an end and, like labels, they have the least possible connection with the event." The greater the leader, "the more conspicuous the inevitability and the predestination of every act he commits." The leader, said Tolstoy, is "the slave of history."

Determinism takes many forms. Marxism is the determinism of class. Nazism the determinism of race. But the idea of men and women as the slaves of history runs athwart the deepest human instincts. Rigid determinism abolishes the idea of human freedom—

the assumption of free choice that underlies every move we make, every word we speak, every thought we think. It abolishes the idea of human responsibility, since it is manifestly unfair to reward or punish people for actions that are by definition beyond their control. No one can live consistently by any deterministic creed. The Marxist states prove this themselves by their extreme susceptibility to the cult of leadership.

More than that, history refutes the idea that individuals make no difference. In December 1931 a British politician crossing Park Avenue in New York City between 76th and 77th Streets around 10:30 P.M. looked in the wrong direction and was knocked down by an automobile—a moment, he later recalled, of a man aghast, a world aglare: "I do not understand why I was not broken like an eggshell or squashed like a gooseberry." Fourteen months later an American politician, sitting in an open car in Miami, Florida, was fired on by an assassin; the man beside him was hit. Those who believe that individuals make no difference to history might well ponder whether the next two decades would have been the same had Mario Constasino's car killed Winston Churchill in 1931 and Giuseppe Zangara's bullet killed Franklin Roosevelt in 1933. Suppose, in addition, that Adolf Hitler had been killed in the street fighting during the Munich *Putsch* of 1923 and that Lenin had died of typhus during World War I. What would the 20th century be like now?

For better or for worse, individuals do make a difference. "The notion that a people can run itself and its affairs anonymously," wrote the philosopher William James, "is now well known to be the silliest of absurdities. Mankind does nothing save through initiatives on the part of inventors, great or small, and imitation by the rest of us—these are the sole factors in human progress. Individuals of genius show the way, and set the patterns, which common people then adopt and follow."

Leadership, James suggests, means leadership in thought as well as in action. In the long run, leaders in thought may well make the greater difference to the world. But, as Woodrow Wilson once said, "Those only are leaders of men, in the general eye, who lead in action. . . . It is at their hands that new thought gets its translation into the crude language of deeds." Leaders in thought often invent in solitude and obscurity, leaving to later generations the tasks of imitation. Leaders in action—the leaders portrayed in this series—have to be effective in their own time.

And they cannot be effective by themselves. They must act in response to the rhythms of their age. Their genius must be adapted, in a phrase of William James's, "to the receptivities of the moment." Leaders are useless without followers. "There goes the mob," said the French politician hearing a clamor in the streets. "I am their leader. I must follow them." Great leaders turn the inchoate emotions of the mob to purposes of their own. They seize on the opportunities of their time, the hopes, fears, frustrations, crises, potentialities. They succeed when events have prepared the way for them, when the community is awaiting to be aroused, when they can provide the clarifying and organizing ideas. Leadership ignites the circuit between the individual and the mass and thereby alters history.

It may alter history for better or for worse. Leaders have been responsible for the most extravagant follies and most monstrous crimes that have beset suffering humanity. They have also been vital in such gains as humanity has made in individual freedom, religious and racial tolerance, social justice, and respect for human rights.

There is no sure way to tell in advance who is going to lead for good and who for evil. But a glance at the gallery of men and women in *World Leaders—Past and Present* suggests some useful tests.

One test is this: Do leaders lead by force or by persuasion? By command or by consent? Through most of history leadership was exercised by the divine right of authority. The duty of followers was to defer and to obey. "Theirs not to reason why / Theirs but to do and die." On occasion, as with the so-called enlightened despots of the 18th century in Europe, absolutist leadership was animated by humane purposes. More often, absolutism nourished the passion for domination, land, gold, and conquest and resulted in tyranny.

The great revolution of modern times has been the revolution of equality. The idea that all people should be equal in their legal condition has undermined the old structure of authority, hierarchy, and deference. The revolution of equality has had two contrary effects on the nature of leadership. For equality, as Alexis de Tocqueville pointed out in his great study *Democracy in America*, might mean equality in servitude as well as equality in freedom.

"I know of only two methods of establishing equality in the political world," Tocqueville wrote. "Rights must be given to every citizen, or none at all to anyone . . . save one, who is the master of all." There was no middle ground "between the sovereignty of all and the absolute power of one man." In his astonishing prediction of 20th-century totalitarian dictatorship, Tocqueville explained how the revolution of equality could lead to the *"Führerprinzip"* and more terrible absolutism than the world had ever known.

But when rights are given to every citizen and the sovereignty of all is established, the problem of leadership takes a new form, becomes more exacting than ever before. It is easy to issue commands and enforce them by the rope and the stake, the concentration camp and the *gulag.* It is much harder to use argument and achievement to overcome opposition and win consent. The Founding Fathers of the United States understood the difficulty. They believed that history had given them the opportunity to decide, as Alexander Hamilton wrote in the first Federalist Paper, whether men are indeed capable of basing government on "reflection and choice, or whether they are forever destined to depend . . . on accident and force."

Government by reflection and choice called for a new style of leadership and a new quality of followership. It required leaders to be responsive to popular concerns, and it required followers to be active and informed participants in the process. Democracy does not eliminate emotion from politics; sometimes it fosters demagoguery; but it is confident that, as the greatest of democratic leaders put it, you cannot fool all of the people all of the time. It measures leadership by results and retires those who overreach or falter or fail.

It is true that in the long run despots are measured by results too. But they can postpone the day of judgment, sometimes indefinitely, and in the meantime they can do infinite harm. It is also true that democracy is no guarantee of virtue and intelligence in government, for the voice of the people is not necessarily the voice of God. But democracy, by assuring the right of opposition, offers built-in resistance to the evils inherent in absolutism. As the theologian Reinhold Niebuhr summed it up, "Man's capacity for justice makes democracy possible, but man's inclination to injustice makes democracy necessary."

A second test for leadership is the end for which power is sought. When leaders have as their goal the supremacy of a master race or the promotion of totalitarian revolution or the acquisition and exploitation of colonies or the protection of greed and privilege or the preservation of personal power, it is likely that their leadership will do little to advance the cause of humanity. When their goal is the abolition of slavery, the liberation of women, the enlargement of opportunity for the poor and powerless, the extension of equal rights to racial minorities, the defense of the freedoms of expression and opposition, it is likely that their leadership will increase the sum of human liberty and welfare.

Leaders have done great harm to the world. They have also conferred great benefits. You will find both sorts in this series. Even "good" leaders must be regarded with a certain wariness. Leaders are not demigods; they put on their trousers one leg after another just like ordinary mortals. No leader is infallible, and every leader needs to be reminded of this at regular intervals. Irreverence irritates leaders but is their salvation. Unquestioning submission corrupts leaders and demeans followers. Making a cult of a leader is always a mistake. Fortunately hero worship generates its own antidote. "Every hero," said Emerson, "becomes a bore at last."

The signal benefit the great leaders confer is to embolden the rest of us to live according to our own best selves, to be active, insistent, and resolute in affirming our own sense of things. For great leaders attest to the reality of human freedom against the supposed inevitabilities of history. And they attest to the wisdom and power that may lie within the most unlikely of us, which is why Abraham Lincoln remains the supreme example of great leadership. A great leader, said Emerson, exhibits new possibilities to all humanity. "We feed on genius. . . . Great men exist that there may be greater men."

Great leaders, in short, justify themselves by emancipating and empowering their followers. So humanity struggles to master its destiny, remembering with Alexis de Tocqueville: "It is true that around every man a fatal circle is traced beyond which he cannot pass; but within the wide verge of that circle he is powerful and free; as it is with man, so with communities."

1

"We Are in Control"

We are in control of the situation," Philippine president Ferdinand Edralin Marcos told his nation on television on February 25, 1986. "Famous last words," quipped a Manila shopkeeper. A moment later, as if in response to the merchant's gibe, the image of Marcos blinked twice and then disappeared from the screen as the state-controlled television station capitulated to rebel forces.

As long as Marcos remained in control of the country's media, not to mention its banks, armed forces, and government agencies, he could rephrase any defeat as a victory. For decades, he had made reality simply by proclaiming it. By declaring himself a war hero, he had become one. By proclaiming that he had won the presidential election, he thought that he did win it. With the fall of the television station, however, the president lost his power to create the "truth" by proclamation.

Two and a half weeks earlier, on February 7, Marcos had run in an election against an extremely popular opponent, Corazon Aquino. As the world watched through the eyes of a vast and vigilant foreign press corps, government forces used violence

> *I am the president. They are not going to drive me out because the people are behind me.*
> —FERDINAND MARCOS
> Feb. 1986

Ferdinand Edralin Marcos, president of the Philippines, speaks at one of the last press conferences he held in office, six days before the presidential election of February 1986. The election pitted the powerful Marcos against a politically inexperienced but popular opponent, Corazon Aquino.

A National Assembly official displays an empty ballot box during the vote counting for the 1986 election. Despite overwhelming evidence of fraud, the assembly declared Marcos the victor.

to intimidate the people, stole and stuffed ballot boxes, bribed voters, and did whatever they could to stack the results in Marcos's favor. Despite the cheating, when the official tabulation bureau started counting the votes, Aquino led by a decisive margin. In a final and desperate attempt to win the election, government agents simply ordered the vote counters to change the results to favor Marcos.

But now, after 20 years, the undeniable truth was asserting itself against Marcos's deceptions and manipulations. At the same time, the Philippine people were asserting themselves and their demands as hundreds of thousands of students, peasants, street urchins, business people, priests, and nuns defied government curfews and flooded the streets of the capital city of Manila in a show of support for Aquino and the opposition.

"We are in control of the situation." The words made up one of Marcos's last public messages before three U.S. helicopters swooped out of the dark tropical sky and plucked him, his family, and an entourage of supporters from the presidential palace to a life of exile.

Before the Spanish arrived in the 16th century, the peoples of the Philippine islands had little more in common with each other than the seas that kept them apart. The range of ethnic backgrounds and cultural practices on the more than 7,100 islands was vast. The earliest inhabitants, Negrito and Malay peoples probably from the Asian continent, were influenced by Indian, Arab, and Indonesian merchants who traveled to the archipelago and began trading goods at the start of the Christian era. By the 10th century, the Chinese were actively trading among the islands, and they were joined by Japanese merchants about five centuries later. To the islands of the Sulu archipelago in the south, Indonesians brought Islam, the religion of Mohammed, and by the late 15th century, Muslims predominated in the south. In the dense mountains of central Luzon, the largest island of the Philippines, the Kalinga tribe practiced head-hunting. Just to the south of the Kalingas were the Ifugaos, architects of the world's most incredible rice terraces. About 100 distinct tribes inhabited the islands, and even in the early 1980s, 70 different languages were still spoken in the Philippines.

In about 200 B.C. a group of Malayan immigrants had come north from Borneo through the southwestern Philippine islands of Palawan and Mindoro to Luzon, where they had settled mainly on the northwest coast in what is now known as the province of Ilocos Norte. These people, famous for their industriousness, frugality, and hardiness, pushed the weaker tribes they encountered into the interior

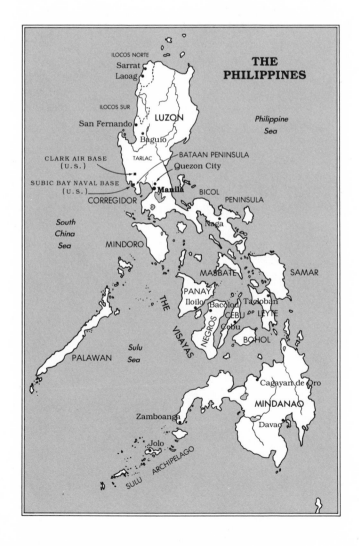

The Philippines is an archipelago in the South Pacific made up of more than 7,100 islands. Many different peoples, including Arabs, Chinese, Indonesians, and Indians settled alongside the native Malay and Negrito tribes.

15

of the island. Among these tough Ilocanos were the ancestors of Ferdinand Marcos.

The Philippine islands were not considered a single territory until the Spanish named them in honor of their king, Philip II, in the mid-16th century. The islands had been discovered in 1521 when Ferdinand Magellan, a Portuguese seafarer working for Spain, had sailed into the group of central Philippine islands now called the Visayan Islands. Magellan, whose job was to find new territories for Spain, had accidentally run into a tropical paradise. Lying about 1,000 miles southeast of China, the Philippines would become a great trading colony where the wealth of China could be funneled to Spain through the annual galleon to Mexico. On the nearby island of Mactan, Magellan erected a cross and claimed the region for Spain. But Lapu-Lapu, a proud and possessive native chief, was not ready to turn his authority over to a king from a land he had never seen. The ensuing battle ended in Magellan's death and the temporary retreat of the Spanish.

In 1565 the Spanish conqueror Miguel López de Legazpi sailed to the islands and forged an alliance with a powerful island ruler, Rajah Sikatuna. With the rajah's help Legazpi conquered the Visayan island of Cebu and erected the first Spanish settlement in the Philippines. In 1571 he conquered Manila and a year later the northern region of the islands. The Spanish then went to work converting the Filipinos to Christianity.

The Augustinians, a Catholic order of priests, had come with Legazpi, and others followed. The orders' priests, or friars, soon held considerable control over local populations. Although the friars eventually were supposed to give up their positions as religious leaders to secular priests — native Filipino priests who did not belong to an order — most of them wanted to hold on to the land and the power they enjoyed. Their missionary efforts were very successful: By the 1800s most Filipinos were baptized Christians. However, Filipinos layered Christianity over religious practices and beliefs that had been part of their cultures for thousands of years. Some

Portuguese adventurer Ferdinand Magellan sailed under the Spanish flag when he discovered the Philippine islands in 1521. After angry natives killed Magellan, the Spanish did not attempt a permanent settlement until 1565.

FERNAND, MAGELLAN,

FERNAND MAGELLAN.

Members of the Tasaday tribe on the island of Mindanao in 1972. Approximately 100 separate tribal groups can be found in the Philippines, and many live apart from modern civilization. The Tasaday, one of the most primitive tribes, exhibit what has been described as a Stone Age culture.

of the island's natives even called themselves Catholics while maintaining their traditional head-hunting practices and cannibalism rites.

The Spanish were ruthless colonizers, holding most of the islands' valuable agricultural land, wringing taxes out of the local populations, and providing little in the way of government. However, a class of relatively wealthy and powerful Spanish-Filipinos emerged by the middle of the 18th century. (A class of Chinese-Filipino elite, whose wealth came from trade, already existed.) These *mestizos* (from the Spanish for crossbreeding) became a kind of puppet government for the Spanish, enforcing the policies of the governor in exchange for permission to go into business or farm plantations. The colonial authorities allowed the mestizos considerable control over their own localities.

Many of the wealthy mestizo families sent their children to be educated in Europe, especially in Spain. In the second half of the 19th century, these young Filipinos became attracted to the growing nationalist movements of Europe. Filipinos eagerly adopted the ideas of self-determination and independence and began to agitate for the overthrow of the Spanish colonial government in the Philippines.

The most important of the Philippine nationalist revolutionaries was the scientist and writer José Rizal y Mercado, who came from a rich Chinese mestizo family and studied in Spain. After writing books

In the mid-16th century, Spanish explorers claimed the Philippines for Spain, naming the country in honor of King Philip II. Among the Spanish were Catholic missionaries, who would have a profound influence on Philippine culture.

PHILIPPE II.
Roy d'Espagne

17

Nationalist Emilio Aguinaldo (on horse) founded Katipunan, an organization dedicated to the overthrow of Spanish colonial rule in the Philippines. In 1896 his secret society launched an unsuccessful revolution.

condemning Spanish colonial rule in the Philippines, Rizal returned to his homeland in 1892 and established a branch of his *Liga Filipina*, the Philippine League, which he had founded a year earlier to promote his country's independence.

At the same time as the Philippine League was expanding, a proindependence organization known as Katipunan set out on a more violent road to national freedom. Led by Emilio Aguinaldo, the secret society launched a revolution in August 1896. Despite having no connection with the Katipunan revolt, Rizal was arrested as an accomplice and executed in late December. His death triggered more anti-Spanish sentiment.

The Filipinos' struggle against the Spanish government received an unexpected boost with the outbreak of the Spanish-American War of 1898. The war began because of U.S. concerns about Cuba, where anti-Spanish rebels had launched a revolt in 1895. The Cubans' war for independence attracted a lot of sympathy in the United States and was a cause of concern for U.S. business interests on the island. In February 1898 the U.S. battleship *Maine* was rocked by an explosion in Havana harbor that sank the ship and took the lives of 260 men. Outraged by the sinking, for which they blamed the Spanish, Americans threw their support to the Cuban rebels. President William McKinley formally declared war on Spain on April 25 and ordered troops sent to Cuba.

The first battle of the war, however, was fought on the other side of the world. Upon being informed of the declaration of war, George Dewey, commander of the U.S. Asiatic squadron, sailed south from Hong Kong, and on May 1 he destroyed the outmoded Spanish fleet in Manila Bay. The first U.S. troops arrived in the Philippines in July, and fighting together, the Americans and the rebel Filipinos, led by Aguinaldo, captured Manila and defeated the Spanish. After suffering several defeats in Cuba, some with heavy loss of life, Spain surrendered in July.

Aguinaldo, who had set up a provisional republic in June, prepared for independence. The Filipino revolutionaries were jubilant over the defeat of Spain, but their joy turned to shock when they heard the terms of the peace treaty. The United States bought the Philippines (along with the Pacific island of Guam and the Caribbean island of Puerto Rico) from Spain for $20 million. Aguinaldo's revolutionary government had not even been consulted. After suffering for centuries under Spanish rule, Filipinos now found they had merely traded one master for another.

The Filipinos' refusal to relinquish their newly won independence led to the Philippine-American War. The war was long and bitter, marked by atrocities on both sides, and left deep scars on the Philippine national consciousness. In a hard-fought guerrilla war Filipino nationalists battled the militarily superior United States until 1902. In the south the Muslims, or Moros as they were called, continued to fight. The United States maintained a military government in the southern part of the country until the last of the Muslim resistance was put down in late 1913.

A U.S. Marine detachment stands at attention as the first U.S. flag is raised in the Philippines in 1898. The victorious United States bought the country from Spain after the Spanish-American War, much to the dismay of the Filipinos, who had hoped for independence.

By 1917, when Ferdinand Marcos was born, the United States was firmly established as the occupying force of the Philippines. Despite their ruthlessness during the Philippine-American War, Americans did a far more humane job of ruling the islands than the Spanish had before them. Schools were set up, and American missionary teachers energetically went about teaching Filipino children English, math, and history. Millions of U.S. dollars were spent building roads, a telephone service, and a railroad. These systems were a great aid to government administrators and propelled the economy toward modernization by allowing the distribution of food, timber, minerals, and other resources around the country. The new transportation systems also aided American businessmen in getting the islands' valuable raw goods, such as hemp, gold, and sugar, onto ships bound for the United States. In turn these businessmen distributed and sold manufactured goods made in the United States to millions of Filipinos.

The Americans established a colonial government run by Filipinos under the direction and ultimate authority of the United States. The United States also appeased the liberty-hungry Filipinos with the promise of eventual independence. Most Filipinos became convinced that American rule was not so bad; at least it was much better than Spanish rule had been under the corrupt friars. But still, the Filipinos longed for freedom.

Ferdinand Edralin Marcos was born on September 11, 1917, in Sarrat, a small village in the northern province of Ilocos Norte on Luzon. Since the 1850s, both the Marcoses and the Edralins (Ferdinand's mother's family) had enjoyed a privileged status as members of the middle class; they were landowners, educated, and considered among the most prominent Filipinos in Ilocos Norte.

Ferdinand was part of the new generation of Americanized Filipinos. His father, Mariano, taught in an American-run school, and he made sure that his son was well versed in English, American history, and American political philosophy. During Ferdinand's childhood this Americanism was balanced by his maternal grandfather, Fructuoso Edralin. Grandfather Edralin was a follower of Gregorio Aglipay, a revolutionary Catholic priest who had fought passionately against both Spanish and U.S. rule in the Philippines. In 1902 Aglipay established the *Iglesia Filipina Independiente*, the Independent Philippine church, in which Filipinos held positions equivalent to those occupied only by Spanish priests in the Catholic church. Aglipay also incorporated native Filipino beliefs and customs into his church. Ferdinand grew up in this peculiar nationalistic and religious environment.

Even more influential on the young Ferdinand than the nationalistic mysticism of Aglipayanism was the intense political atmosphere of his home. Mariano Marcos represented the Aglipay faction in the Philippine congress in 1924 and 1928. The Marcos home was a constant river of constituents, political allies, and lobbyists. It was an exciting atmosphere for a precocious child such as Ferdinand, who absorbed the thrill of elections, the intense craving for victory, and the fear of defeat.

Mariano taught Ferdinand and his younger brother, Pacifico, to box, wrestle, and shoot. The emphasis, however, was not on sportsmanship but on victory. He often told his sons, "Don't start a fight until you know you can win it." Ferdinand's father was also a firm believer in strict self-discipline. Once when Ferdinand cut himself while playing and ran to his father for sympathy, Mariano refused to console the boy and responded with anger instead, saying, "A Marcos never cries; no self-pity, son."

Josefa Edralin Marcos, Ferdinand's mother, came from one of the wealthiest families in Ilocos. Her part-Chinese parents owned huge tobacco plantations in the southern part of the region. But Josefa did not spoil her children. They were forced to take care of themselves. It is said that she told Ferdinand, his two sisters, and his brother that they had to earn scholarships to attend school. Victor Nituda, a Marcos biographer, wrote that it is "to his mother [that] President Marcos owes the desire to excel so fierce that, if at all, it is hard for him to accept being second to anyone in anything."

> *Even discounting the mythmaking and boasting, Marcos's accomplishments [in his youth] were extraordinary. Even if he wasn't the outstanding athlete of his time, he was certainly a valued member of the university's wrestling, boxing, and swimming teams and captain of the rifle and pistol team.*
> —RAYMOND BONNER
> American journalist

A jubilant crowd cheers Emilio Aguinaldo in his bid for president of the Philippine commonwealth in 1935. After being promised independence by the United States, many Filipinos, including the Marcos family, became involved in the intensely emotional national politics of the 1930s.

This drive to be the best made Marcos an exceptional student. He won scholarships to attend the University of the Philippines, in Manila, where he studied law. In 1935 Ferdinand took a holiday from law school and returned to Ilocos Norte for the Philippines' first legislative elections under the new commonwealth status granted by the American colonizers. The previous year, the U.S. Congress had passed the Tydings-McDuffie Act, which provided for a self-governing Philippine commonwealth for a period of 10 years as a transition to full independence. The direction of foreign affairs and the military remained in U.S. hands. A new legislature, the National Assembly, and a new president were to be elected. Mariano Marcos decided to run for a congressional seat against a popular local official, Julio Nalundasan.

There was more at issue in this election than just the worthiness of the two candidates to represent their district in congress. Because Mariano Marcos represented the Aglipay faction whereas Nalundasan was backed by the more traditional Catholic constituency, the campaign was also a pivotal battle in an old religious feud. Aglipayanism's political influence had weakened during the years of American occupation, and it was struggling for its survival. If Aglipay's supporters failed to win seats in the national assembly, the native movement would be finished as a political force in the islands.

Nalundasan won the election by a wide margin, killing any hopes that Mariano Marcos or Aglipay would regain a position of political power. After the election results came in, Nalundasan's supporters held a victory parade past the Marcos house. Two coffins, mounted on the back of an automobile, held men marked "Marcos" and "Aglipay." In front of the Marcos family the victors pretended to mourn, wailing and wiping away false tears.

During the next night, September 20, rain poured down in sheets. By 10:30 P.M. the town's streets were empty except for someone with a rifle, evil intentions, and very good aim. Nalundasan's house was only a few minutes' walk from the Marcos home. Nalundasan had returned home late after a day spent celebrating his victory. He stood on an enclosed porch brushing his teeth and preparing for bed when a shot rang out. Nalundasan fell to the floor with a bullet in his heart.

Everyone in the small town believed that the murderer was a Marcos. They also knew that young Ferdinand was a crack shot on the University of the Philippines' shooting club.

2

Convict and Hero

The investigation of Nalundasan's murder proceeded slowly. Marcos returned to school in Manila, where he studied hard and dabbled in student politics, even participating in some antigovernment demonstrations.

Three years after the murder, in December 1938, Marcos was a senior expecting to graduate in four short months as class valedictorian (first in the program) and magna cum laude (with high honors). On December 7, the police interrupted an evening class attended by Marcos. "You'll have to come with me," the policeman who burst into the room said to Marcos. "Are you kidding? Can't you see I'm in class?" Marcos answered. The officer curtly replied that he was arresting Marcos for murder.

His arrest put him on the front pages of newspapers across the country and made "Ferdinand Marcos" a household name. Perhaps more importantly it thrust him into the sink-or-swim world of Philippine politics. He learned to connive, use what political connections he had to maximum advantage, and work tirelessly in order to save his career and his life. He learned to transform a disaster into

He [Marcos] deeply impressed the court whenever he took an active part in the defense of his own case.
—trial judge at Marcos's trial

In 1938 Ferdinand Marcos was a brilliant young law student with a promising future when he suddenly found himself under arrest for the murder of his father's political rival. His imprisonment and trial gave him a hard lesson in Philippine politics.

a political asset. He also discovered the power of popular opinion and how to manipulate it through the media. The lessons Marcos learned during his trial for murder prepared him for his remarkable rise to power.

That December night in 1938, Marcos was taken from the university and brought back to Ilocos Norte. At the station house in Laoag he was charged with the murder of Nalundasan and locked in a small cell. Also arrested for the murder were Marcos's father, his uncle Pio, and his uncle Quirino Lizardo. They were all charged with conspiracy to kill Nalundasan, but young Ferdinand was accused of pulling the trigger.

No one doubted that the Marcoses were responsible for the crime, but hard evidence was lacking. It had been three years since the murder, but the local prosecutor was under tremendous pressure from the national government to solve the crime and show the United States and the world that Filipinos could take care of their own affairs and turn their own wheels of justice.

Marcos had so much confidence that he was not really afraid of conviction. But he did fear spending time in prison waiting to be acquitted. How would he be able to finish law school and take the bar exams while in prison? He lobbied everyone he knew with any clout at all to help convince the judge in Laoag that he deserved to be released on bail so he could finish his classes and take his exams. His supporters petitioned the judge, saying that it would be a tragedy if the life of this young and talented law student was wasted on just the basis of accusation. After two months in jail, Marcos was released on bail. His trial was scheduled to take place in September. By then Marcos would be finished with law school and would have taken his bar exams.

Not surprisingly, Marcos lost some of his usual enthusiasm living under the cloud of his approaching trial. But he kept busy studying, and he refused to give in to despair even when more problems compounded the scandal. In April 1939, one week before

While studying for the bar exam, he boasted that he would have the highest scores. He did, the accomplishment all the more remarkable considering that he must surely have been distracted by the arrest and murder charges hanging over him.

—RAYMOND BONNER
American journalist

commencement, the president of the University of the Philippines informed Marcos that he would not be allowed to graduate. The university required that any student who missed more than three weeks of class be dismissed. The time Marcos had spent in jail, the president said, disqualified him from graduating.

By now Marcos was a celebrity, and his defense was a popular cause on campus. Students and law professors met the president's decision with vocal protests and demanded that he change his ruling. Marcos was allowed to graduate, though he was stripped of his valedictorian status.

The Philippine national legislature in Manila was a hotbed of activity in the preindependence years. The commonwealth government saw the Marcos murder case as a perfect opportunity to prove to the United States that Filipinos had mastered a democratic judicial system.

Marcos and his codefendants retained Vicente Francisco to prepare their case. Always looking for an opportunity to advance himself, Marcos added a practical touch to his legal education by working alongside Francisco, considered the best trial attorney in the Philippines at that time, in the preparation of the legal brief used in his family's defense.

Marcos toiled through the hot, rainy summer in Laoag. He had always been a good student and a hard worker, but now his life depended on his efforts, and he devoted himself to research. At this time he discovered that if he took short, frequent naps during the day he needed only a few hours sleep each night. Then he could work long into the quiet and productive hours of the predawn morning. He would keep this long working schedule throughout his political career until his health failed.

In addition to helping his attorney prepare the defense, Marcos also had to prepare himself for the

The main lecture hall at the University of the Philippines in Manila, where Marcos studied law. In November 1939, officials accused him of cheating on the bar exam, claiming that his scores were too high. To prove them wrong, Marcos took an oral exam in which he astonished them with his mastery of the law.

The Marcos family retained Vicente Francisco, a prominent trial attorney, to present their case in court. The trial would be one of the most sensational events in the history of Philippine law.

bar exam. He had spent months of valuable class time languishing in prison and needed to make up for it. He feared that he would fail the important exam and thus ruin any chance of a prominent legal career. In public, though, Marcos boasted that he would earn the highest scores of anyone on the bar exams.

When Marcos finally took the exams in August 1939 he worried because he finished so much earlier than the other students, reports his official biographer, Hartzell Spence. He was concerned about the exams, but it would be months before the results were returned, and he had the trial to think about.

The Nalundasan murder trial began on September 7 with the prosecution presenting a case based on testimony by Calixo Aguinaldo, a man who claimed to have been Lizardo's bodyguard and chauffeur during the election and the subsequent murder. He testified that he had heard the Marcos clan conspiring to kill Nalundasan if he won the election. He said he had driven Ferdinand and Lizardo to the victim's house the night of the killing. The Marcoses, for their part, denied that they even knew the accuser and countercharged that he was hired as a witness. Their defense strategy was to discredit Aguinaldo and demonstrate that without his testimony there was no real case against them.

After two long months of trial the court finally recessed. While he was waiting for the judge to decide the verdict, Marcos suffered yet another blow. On November 29, he was summoned to the office of the law school dean. The dean accused his former student of the serious crime of cheating on the bar exam. Ferdinand's score was simply too high, the dean said. He had scored 100 in criminal law; 100 in legal ethics; 100 in international law; 98 in civil law; 97 in commercial law; 97 in procedural law; and 95 in political law, for an average of just more than 98. His accuser demanded to know how Marcos had obtained copies of the questions in advance.

Marcos was stunned by the humiliating allegation. He boldly suggested that the dean call a board of law professors together on the spot to give him an oral exam. The professors fired seemingly impossible questions at him in rapid-fire succession. Marcos answered promptly, citing chapters from the law books. They were astounded by his mastery of the subjects and, more important, they were convinced that he had legitimately earned his high marks on the bar exam.

A great celebration followed the announcement of Marcos's all-time high score. Biographer Spence reports that a crowd of 8,000 gathered for the bonfire party held in Marcos's honor by his alma mater. The president of the university, who had tried to prevent Marcos from graduating only a couple of months earlier, congratulated him for bringing prestige to the school as well as glory to himself. The dean, who had stood as Marcos's accuser only hours before, was cheery now as he described Marcos's brilliant performance during the impromptu oral exam.

But the crowd had come to hear Marcos. When he rose to speak in the light of the bonfire he told the crowd that one of the most important tasks faced by the members of his generation was to drive

After Marcos's dramatic Supreme Court acquittal, Philippine president Manuel Quezon (seated, center, with his family) offered him a choice judicial post in his government. Marcos, however, refused to join the people who had been his persecutors.

out corrupt public officials who could falsely accuse or condemn anyone. On a lighter but no less ironic note, he said that the lowest score he got on the exams was in political law. He quipped to the appreciative audience: "I guess that proves that I have no future in politics. So, I will have to practice law without the appendage of being a politician." Toward the end of his speech, Marcos was interrupted by the siren of an approaching police car. As two agents got out of the jeep and walked up to the platform the audience hushed. The verdict was in, and Marcos's bail had been rescinded. At the height of his glory he was thrown in jail once again.

Mariano and Pio Marcos were acquitted, but Ferdinand and Quirino Lizardo were found guilty; Lizardo was sentenced to life imprisonment. Ferdinand received a sentence of 17 years and 4 months. It was a terrible blow. Whether he was guilty or not, he had been utterly convinced that he, the nation's most promising law student, would not be convicted. He had worked so hard; could it all have been wasted? Of the verdict, Spence wrote, "Something died in Marcos at that moment. He was never known to be completely carefree again."

But he did not give up. Though the family fortune had all been spent on the trial, Marcos took the legal battle to the Supreme Court. Before he had appealed the lower court's decision, however, he was approached by the presiding judge, who said he was recommending a pardon in Marcos's case. Marcos was not grateful; on the contrary, he was incensed. According to Spence, Marcos declared, "I will never accept any such favor as this. Further, why should I live under the stigma of a pardon, which implies my guilt? No, I will appeal to the supreme court and prove my innocence." During his time in prison he prepared his own briefs to plead his innocence before the court.

Marcos was the youngest person ever to present a case to the nation's highest court. The trial was a sensation, and the scandal-loving Philippine press exploited it fully. Marcos appeared before the Supreme Court in a white double-breasted sharkskin suit and white shoes that contrasted sharply with the black attire normally worn in the Philippine courts. His case, outlined in a brief that totaled 830 pages, contained 4 basic points. First, he argued, the court had erred in freeing Mariano and Pio while convicting the other two defendants on the same charges. Second, the court should not have accepted the testimony of Calixo Aguinaldo, whom the defense had managed to discredit, over that of the testimony and alibis of the reputable Marcos family. Third, Marcos argued, the court should have given some acknowledgment of the defense's proof that Aguinaldo was 300 miles away at the time he said he was witnessing the conspiracy to kill Nalundasan. Finally, he contended, if Aguinaldo's testimony was accurate, the witness should also have been charged with conspiracy and with aiding and abetting the crime.

The presiding judge was either convinced by Marcos's arguments or persuaded by a combination of Marcos's intelligence and public sympathy for him. He acquitted Marcos and Lizardo. Marcos won the innocent verdict for which he had fought. Two Manila newspapers printed extra editions to proclaim his victory. The *Philippine Free Press* put Marcos

After Marcos was convicted of murder, he decided to argue his own case before the Philippine Supreme Court. The presiding judge was José Laurel, shown here, whose decisions in Marcos's favor would benefit him and his family several years later.

on its cover and, even though he was not yet an attorney, crowned him "Lawyer of the Year." It said of Marcos that this "bright, boyish, buoyant 23-year-old metamorphosed overnight from a convicted murderer into a public hero."

If there was a metamorphosis, however, it was in legal status and public perception only. Marcos was free, but his spirit was still imprisoned by the bitterness of his experience. The trial, and the politics surrounding it, were his first good look into the corrupt systems of Philippine government, which operated on the currency of bribes and personal influence. Marcos had learned to fight and win. He had also found in himself an incredible and powerful ability to stretch the truth.

The experience made him bitter and ambitious for revenge. When he was acquitted, President Manuel Quezon offered him a job as chief prosecutor for the Philippine Department of Investigation. It would have been a prestigious position for a student fresh out of law school. Marcos turned it down. He refused to work for the same administration that had prosecuted him. He decided that, one way or another, he would eventually make the administration work for him instead. Rather than give in to the bitterness, Marcos transformed it into the energy that fueled his pursuit of power.

Malacañang Palace in Manila was the home of the Philippine president. After the disillusionment of his trial, Marcos decided that the presidency would be his ultimate goal, and he single-mindedly set out to achieve the power he desired.

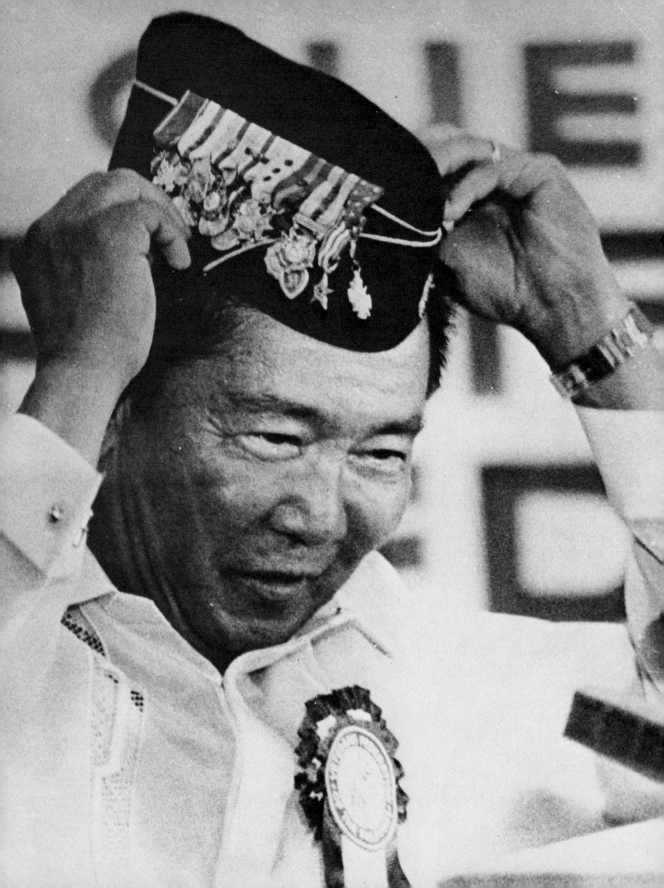

3

Hero or Liar?

The most traumatic event in 20th-century Philippine history was the brutal invasion and occupation of the islands by Japan during World War II. On December 7, 1941, 11 hours after their surprise attack on the U.S. naval fleet at Pearl Harbor, Hawaii, the Japanese landed troops in the Philippines.

General Douglas MacArthur, commander of the U.S. armed forces in the Far East, headed the defending Filipino and American troops. The defenders found themselves in a hopeless situation: The Japanese had destroyed all the U.S. aircraft on the ground; the ships anchored in the Philippines were ordered to leave in order to avoid attack; and no reinforcements could be expected from the debilitated forces in Hawaii. Manila was proclaimed an open city, that is, one that would not resist the invaders, in order to avoid total destruction. The Japanese occupied it on January 2, 1942. General MacArthur was unable to stem the invasion, and most of his troops retreated to the Bataan Peninsula in southwestern Luzon. Some went to the tiny island of Corregidor at the mouth of Manila Bay to carry on what last resistance they could.

According to Spence, whose primary source for his adulatory biography was Marcos himself, both Marcos and his brother had been reserve officers in

If Marcos stretched the truth about his early life, it snapped when he recounted his military years.
—RAYMOND BONNER
American journalist

Marcos proudly displays his military cap and World War II medals before a Filipino veterans' group in 1982. Marcos built up political power on his record as a war hero, but his boastful claims were later proved to be gross exaggerations.

U.S. general Douglas Mac-Arthur (right) talks with General Jonathan Wainwright. MacArthur was in charge of the U.S. and Filipino troops who bravely attempted to stave off the Japanese invasion in 1941. When defeat was imminent, MacArthur went to Australia but vowed to return to the Philippines.

the defense training program established by the United States with an eye toward developing strong, well-trained Filipino armed forces by the time of Philippine independence in 1946. Marcos was called up for duty in November 1941, just before the Japanese invasion, and assigned as a combat intelligence officer. He was among those soldiers on the retreat to Bataan.

The fighting on Bataan continued until the defending troops were exhausted, their supplies gone. They surrendered in April 1942, and with the fall of Corregidor the following month, the Japanese assumed control of the country. Filipinos were shocked. They never thought their powerful North American protectors would succumb to the invader. President Quezon fled to the United States, where he established a government-in-exile. MacArthur, ordered to continue the struggle from Australia, made a solemn vow to the Filipinos: "I shall return."

With the surrender of the U.S.-Filipino forces came one of the worst episodes of brutality in the history of the war in the Pacific. In what was later termed the "Death March," about 75,000 U.S. and Filipino soldiers were forced to walk 65 miles north, across the Bataan Peninsula, to San Fernando. There they were loaded onto freight cars and transported to Capas, in the central Luzon province of Tarlac, where they began an eight-mile march to Camp O'Donnell. The forced march was a horror; the prisoners, many of whom were ill with various tropical diseases or wounded in battle, were given little or no food or water. They were beaten, tortured, or killed along the way. Any man who fell was left to die. Every time a prisoner was caught trying to escape, 10 were shot on the spot. It is estimated that between 7,000 and 10,000 men (of whom perhaps 2,300 were Americans) died on the march alone. When the prisoners arrived at Camp O'Donnell the inhuman treatment continued, and another 29,000 Filipino and American soldiers died there before the camp was closed in March 1943. This shared tragedy brought Filipinos and Americans together in a way both would remember for decades to come.

Marcos survived the Bataan Death March but, according to his official biographer, not by much. By the time he reached Camp O'Donnell he was "black from sunburn, clothed in a shred of trousers and a tatter of polo shirt. He weighed 105 pounds, scarcely enough to hold his bones together. . . . His mouth and throat were so dry that he could not swallow, and he could scarcely breathe." Whatever bitterness remained from Marcos's trial was forged during this horrible period of abuse and torture. Marcos would later call the prison camp "the birthplace of hatred."

Exactly what Marcos did in Camp O'Donnell is not clear, but some soldiers did whatever they could to appease the Japanese, even if that meant spying on or betraying other inmates. In 1942 the prisoners at Camp O'Donnell were released after signing pledges not to fight against the Japanese. Marcos, released on August 4, was extremely ill with gastric ulcer, malaria, and beriberi, a nervous system disease caused by vitamin deficiency. He went to his mother's house in Manila, but he was arrested the following day and taken to Fort Santiago, where he claims he was tortured and interrogated for eight days by the *Kempei Tai* — the Japanese secret police. Pretending to cooperate, Marcos said he led a Japanese search party to a boat anchorage where, according to a secret plan set up by himself and some Filipino guerrillas, the search party was ambushed, and he was freed.

According to Spence, after Marcos's escape he proceeded to engage in action that won him 32 medals, more than anyone else fighting for the Allied nations in World War II. His medals reportedly included two U.S. Silver Stars, the Distinguished Service Cross, and the highly coveted Congressional Medal of Honor. Marcos claims to have played a central role in the victory over Japan. With a company of only 100 guerrillas, according to Spence, Marcos held back 2,000 Japanese invaders and his "heroic stand at Bataan upset the Japanese timetable of conquest, gave the allies time to defend the South Pacific, and thus saved Australia and New Zealand."

Spence and Marcos also claim that Marcos organized and led a guerrilla unit called *Ang Mga Ma-*

The U.S. fleet in Manila Bay, which many Filipinos thought would protect them against the Japanese, was ordered to leave the Philippines in order to avoid the same fate the ships at Pearl Harbor had suffered.

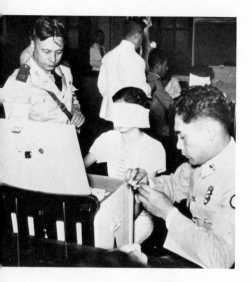

A blindfolded woman draws numbers for Filipinos to be drafted into the armed forces. Marcos was an officer in the U.S.-sponsored Philippine defense training program when he was called up for duty in November 1941, shortly before the Japanese invaded.

harlika ("The Free Men" in Tagalog, the Philippines' official language). Maharlika was supposedly composed of several thousand men who gathered intelligence and conducted sabotage activities from Manila to Pangasinan in north central Luzon to Mindoro, the island southwest of Luzon.

It is an indication of the Filipino people's trust in and admiration for Marcos that his fabulous tales of heroism went unquestioned for most of his career. The first manifestation of doubt appeared in the newspaper *Philippine News* in 1982. Since then, however, the validity of Marcos's medals and the veracity of his incredible tales have been closely scrutinized by investigators and journalists who have found them largely unsupported.

Very little can be said with certainty about Marcos's activities during the war years. The evidence is overwhelming that most, if not all, of Marcos's medals were not earned but were either stolen, bought, or given in return for political favors. There is a scant account in U.S. war records of Marcos's Maharlika unit. What is reported indicates that its membership was not the 8,300 Marcos claimed, but fewer than 100 men. Its military activities were of "very little value."

The U.S. Army conducted an investigation in 1948 and concluded that Marcos's claim to have led a unit of that size was not only "fraudulent" but a "malicious criminal act." Furthermore, Marcos's name is not on official U.S. government lists of Filipinos and Americans who were nominated for Distinguished Service Crosses for their bravery at Bataan. There is likewise no record in the U.S. Army archives of his recommendation for the Congressional Medal of Honor.

Marcos did receive a number of World War II medals from the Philippine government, but under suspicious circumstances. Five of them were granted more than four years after the war was over, when Marcos was a leading member of the House Defense Committee, which influenced the allocation of military spending. In 1963, almost two decades after his alleged heroic acts, Marcos received two Distinguished Conduct Stars, two Distinguished Service Stars, two Gold Cross Medals, and three Wounded Personnel Medals. His critics speculate that because Marcos was then chairman of the Senate Appropriations Committee he may have been granted these medals in exchange for votes favorable to the military brass.

According to Romulo Manriquez, Marcos's commanding officer between November 1944 and March 1945, who was interviewed by Raymond Bonner for his 1987 book *Waltzing with a Dictator*, Marcos's claims of heroism make him the "biggest liar in history." Although Manriquez confirms that Marcos was captured by the Japanese at Bataan in April 1942, he claims that after Marcos's release "he did nothing—he traded in the black market."

In support of this allegation, U.S. Army records indicate that Marcos was arrested during the war by a U.S. Army captain for "illegally collecting money." However, Marcos already enjoyed considerable political influence and was released after an uncharacteristically short term of imprisonment, according to a story questioning Marcos's war record published in the *Washington Post* in January 1986. This same newspaper story reports that Marcos may not only have been less than heroic during the war, but that he may have actively collaborated with the Japanese occupiers, selling them American army surplus goods and equipment.

In sum, Marcos was either the Philippines' bravest and most accomplished war hero or that nation's most prolific and talented liar. Whether Marcos's touted war exploits were real or not, they were for a long time a celebrated part of Philippine history and a tremendously important element in the craftily engineered image that led to his great popularity. For to the degree that the Philippine people were ashamed of those politicians who had collaborated with the Japanese during the war, they were also proud of those who had remained true to the cause. And it was by his identification as the greatest patriot of the Philippines that Marcos was able to make himself a living legend.

Weary Allied prisoners of war carry their wounded comrades into Camp O'Donnell in 1945. This camp was the final destination for the men on the 1942 Bataan Death March, the brutal forced march in which thousands of U.S. and Filipino soldiers died. Marcos barely survived the ordeal.

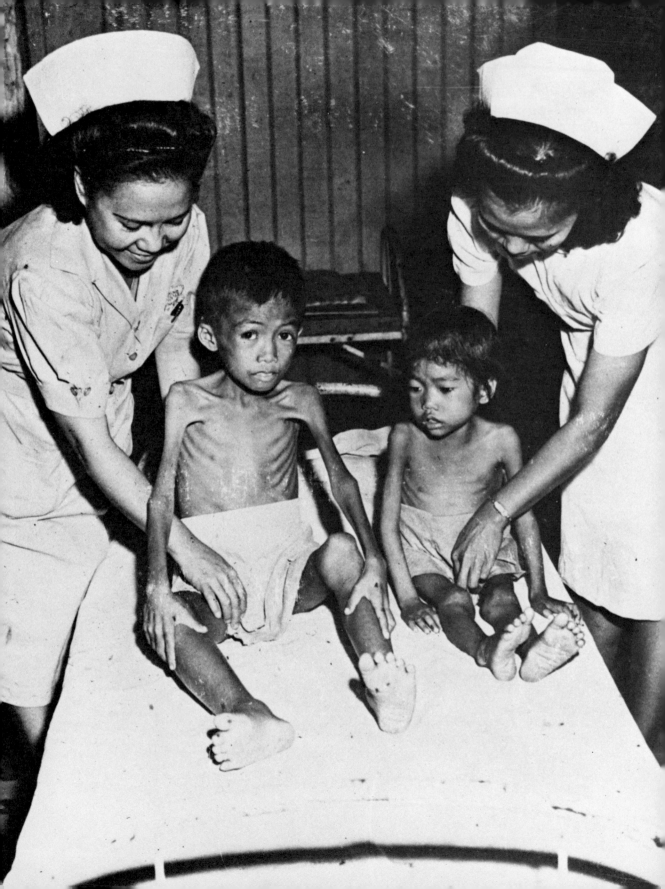

4

First Fortune

On October 20, 1944, General MacArthur fulfilled his promise and returned to the Philippines, landing on the shores of the east Visayan island of Leyte. In bitter fighting, Allied forces drove the Japanese to entrenched positions in northern Luzon and in Manila. Although MacArthur proclaimed the reinstatement of the Philippine commonwealth under the United States in April 1945, another four months of fierce fighting remained before the Japanese commander in the Philippines, General Tomoyuki Yamashita, surrendered. Even then, there were pockets of Japanese resistance up until the surrender of Japan on September 22, 1945. The original timetable for Philippine independence remained in effect, which meant that national independence was only a year away. For Filipinos, the victory was bittersweet. The war was over, and they would shortly have their freedom, but the country was in ruins.

The war had traumatized the Philippines economically, physically, and spiritually. Everything that could be moved was either used by the Japanese during the occupation or taken during the evacuation: Factory and mining machinery, office equipment, even household goods were confiscated and

> *I consider Marcos to be the greatest impostor that World War II has ever produced.*
> —COLONEL ROMULO MANRIQUEZ
> Marcos's commanding officer during World War II

The Japanese invasion and occupation of the Philippines during World War II took a tremendous toll on the country. Widespread destruction left many thousands homeless. With no means of support the population quickly fell prey to starvation and disease.

In October 1944 General MacArthur returned to the Philippines to oversee the defeat of the Japanese. MacArthur announced the restoration of the Philippine commonwealth in April 1945, although pockets of Japanese resistance continued until Japan's final surrender in September 1945.

put to use for the Japanese war effort. Farms were left denuded, their seed and breeding stock eaten. Most of the country's *carabao*, the water buffalo that serve as the main Philippine beast of burden, had been killed. All of the major roads, bridges, and railroads had been destroyed. Public utilities, including sewage and water systems, were inoperative. Most of the schools, libraries, and hospitals had been leveled. Three-quarters of Manila was demolished when the Japanese made a final stand there.

But the material damage was slight compared to the human toll. In addition to the more than 1 million Filipinos killed during the war, the violence had left hundreds of thousands homeless, penniless, and with neither food nor the means to produce it. Widespread starvation and disease posed an immediate, deadly threat.

As if this were not enough, the violence did not end with the defeat of the Japanese. A group of peasant-based guerrillas called the *Hukbalahap* ("The People's Anti-Japanese Army") refused to disband after the war's end. The Huks, as they were known, were formed in 1942 by Luis Tarac, a leading communist. With a total of 30,000 members, they had been the strongest of the resistance guerrilla bands during the war and had controlled several areas in Luzon province. After the war the Huks, most of them peasants, refused to return to work under the unfair economic system, dominated by the landlords on their huge plantations and largely controlled by U.S. interests.

The Huks' anti–United States and egalitarian emphasis, coupled with the communism of many of its leaders, identified it with the left. Consequently, the Huks were not given any representation in the postwar commonwealth government, still under the rule of the United States. Seeing themselves as the true Philippine nationalists, the Huks kept their guerrilla units together and fought the new Philippine government until they were defeated, with help from the United States, in the early 1950s.

The Philippines became an independent republic on July 4, 1946. Marcos joined the Department of

Justice as special advocate of a judicial panel that tried war criminals. But when he discovered that he was to prosecute José Laurel, president of the puppet regime under the Japanese and denounced by many as a blatant collaborator, Marcos resigned. Laurel had been the presiding supreme court judge who acquitted Marcos in the Nalundasan murder trial in 1940. Marcos said he could not prosecute the man who had saved his life.

The young lawyer then went to work handling both criminal and corporate cases for the successful law firm of Vicente Francisco, the defense attorney in his murder case. He still professed to have no interest in pursuing a political career and claimed his highest ambition was to get a doctorate in corporate law from Harvard University in order to become a successful lawyer for the rich and powerful. He resisted invitations to join the administration of Manuel Roxas, the first president of the newly established Republic of the Philippines.

In 1947 Marcos took a job in Washington, D.C., as a member of the four-person Philippines Veterans Commission. His task was to convince U.S. legislators that they should abide by agreements that General MacArthur had made with Filipino soldiers when he retreated from the Philippines. When he left, MacArthur had pledged that those Filipino soldiers who had been on active duty before December 8, 1941, and had continued to fight the Japanese during the occupation would be given back pay and

A displaced Filipino family ride *carabao*, the Philippine beast of burden, to a new home. The carabao, essential to farming, were all but destroyed during the Japanese occupation.

Luis Tarac (center), head of the guerrilla organization known as *Hukbalahap*, or the Huks, poses with his men in 1950 to dispel rumors of his death. After the war, the Huks, who had been the largest anti-Japanese resistance group, fought the injustices of the landlord-dominated economy in the countryside.

other compensation as members of the U.S. armed forces. But the U.S. Congress did not want to add thousands of Filipinos to its budget burden and fought making the Filipino veterans full members of the U.S. armed forces. Marcos had a personal stake in this lobbying effort because he, too, was applying for a military pension for his activities during the war.

The efforts of his commission were successful, and the U.S. Congress finally allocated $160 million to those Filipinos with verifiable claims. It also provided for a Veterans Administration office to be opened in Manila in order to process claims for other veterans' benefits, including education and insurance. Ironically, Marcos's application for back pay was rejected by the U.S. review board on the grounds that he had falsified documents and exaggerated accounts of his military activities during the Japanese occupation.

While in the United States Marcos applied for admission to Harvard University Law School. He was crestfallen when Harvard rejected him: The prestigious university required that in addition to a law degree, Marcos had to have a degree in liberal arts. Sorely disappointed, he returned to the Philippines and went to work for Roxas as technical assistant to the president in his new Economic Development Program. Marcos's assignment was to prepare a survey of the islands' resources and develop strategies for their development and exploitation.

It would be a mistake to attribute Marcos's decision to go into politics to any one motive or another. His rejection by Harvard may have played a part. Probably more importantly, Marcos saw that politics in the independent Philippines was a growth industry ripe for exploitation. New governments needed capable servants, and the traditional Philippine system of patronage, of giving favor for favor, meant that a power base could be built in a short time. In addition, for a lawyer willing to break laws, more money could be made in government than in any other business in the country.

A more generous explanation of Marcos's change of career is described by Spence, who claims that Marcos was persuaded by the popular president Roxas into running for office. Roxas told Marcos that the way to realize his dreams for his country was to enter politics and effect changes. "Only the president has the power to get done what I would like to do," Marcos said. "Then become president," Roxas replied.

To celebrate the forthcoming national independence of the Philippines, wives of government officials hold a "Betsy Ross" party. The U.S. flag these women sewed was raised during the July 4, 1946, independence ceremony held in Manila.

In 1946 Manuel Roxas was elected the first president of the newly independent Republic of the Philippines. Marcos joined his government as a member of a judicial panel that tried war criminals.

Marcos decided to run for congress in his father's old district in Ilocos Norte. He appealed to the people as a fellow Ilocano, promising them that he would aim high: "This is only the first step. Elect me now as congressman and I pledge you an Ilocano president in 20 years, and with that the realization of the dreams we have all fought a war to win." Marcos knew this region well and told the people what they most wanted to hear. He ran on a platform of reform and integrity, denouncing the abuses found in the present system: "True patriotism rests on personal virtue, and nationalism, in the tradition founded by our great heroes, cannot be compatible with systematic corruption and graft." Marcos was a tireless campaigner. Taking little time for sleep and none for recreation, he took his political constituency by storm.

If Marcos went into politics to make money, it was almost immediately clear that he made the right choice. In his first term he authored legislation known as the Import Control Law and became chairman of the committee appointed to implement it. This, his critics allege, is when Marcos made his first fortune. The committee's job was to screen the applications of foreign investors, who would bring in outside currency and sort the worthy applicants from the undesirables. As it turned out, in the process the committee made money for its members. If submitted strictly according to regulations, requests for import licenses could take months to process, even to be denied. For the "cooperative" investor, however, there was a faster way. By offering 10 percent of the proposed investment to a member of the board, the applicant would be guaranteed full rights within 10 days. According to Charles McDougald in his book *The Marcos File*, "Marcos was rumored to be the most notorious ten percenter in the business."

Marcos served three terms in the Philippine House of Representatives. He demonstrated his ability to rally supporters when he forged a coalition of freshmen congressmen who, as long as they stuck together, were able to secure appointments for

themselves on influential committees that were usually reserved for more senior congressmen.

It was during his first years as a congressman that Marcos met the beautiful Carmen Ortega, a former beauty queen, who worked in the import control division of the Central Bank. Ortega moved into Marcos's bungalow in the fashionable Manila section of San Juan, and they had at least one child, though they were never married. Marcos said later that these were the happiest years of his life.

Love is one thing, politics another. Marcos may have loved Ortega, but he was waiting for a more propitious match. He wanted to marry a woman who could give his political career a much-needed boost. When Imelda Romualdez came along in 1954 Marcos left Ortega with hardly a second thought. The Romualdez family was well known. Not only rich and powerful, the Romualdezes were influential in the Visayan Islands, where Marcos's own support was weak. A match between Marcos and Imelda would bring many political supporters. In romance, as in politics, Marcos was a master of immediate action. Once he knew what he wanted, he would stop at nothing to get it. He wanted Imelda.

Filipino workers restore the damaged Luzon railroad as part of a massive government program of postwar economic restoration. Because the Philippines remained heavily dependent on U.S. aid, it allowed its former colonial master an unusual amount of influence in its national economy.

5

Ilocano President

On a balmy April evening in 1954 Imelda Romualdez came to the Philippine House of Representatives to pick up her cousin Danieling Romualdez, the presiding speaker. Danieling left a message for his cousin to meet him in the congressional cafeteria, where Imelda, wearing a plain housedress, chomped away on watermelon seeds as she awaited the speaker.

Congressman Ferdinand Marcos, after spending hours speaking on the House floor, left the chambers and slipped into the cafeteria. There he spotted Imelda for the first time. Imelda considered him too boorish to acknowledge his presence, but Marcos was not daunted. He recruited a mischievous friend who knew the Romualdezes to introduce him to the beauty. Marcos asked Imelda to stand up and then stood with his back to hers. He measured their heads with his hand. Finding that he was a little taller than Imelda (at 5 feet 6 inches she was tall for a Filipino), he said confidently to his friend, "I'm getting married."

They laugh at me when I speak of greatness. But what can I do? I believe in greatness. I believe if one is to have vision, it should be a big vision, a great vision. Otherwise, forget all about vision, go crawl like an insect on the earth, and don't look for vision in the skies.
—FERDINAND MARCOS

Senate president Ferdinand Marcos poses with his wife, Imelda, and their three children, (from left) Irene, Ferdinand, Jr., and Imee. In courting beauty queen Imelda Romualdez, Marcos displayed all the intensity of purpose he brought to politics. The two were married in May 1954, only 11 days after they met.

Imelda was shocked. Although the audacity of this upstart congressman may have impressed her, marriage was out of the question. She was already engaged to Ariston Nakpil, a tall, handsome, and rich, architect. But Marcos was also rich, and, Imelda soon learned from her friends, he promised to get richer still. Moreover, he promised to become very powerful. Imelda, though still cool, began to show a little more interest.

After days of sending Imelda gifts — chocolates, flowers, books, diamonds — Marcos talked the reluctant beauty into riding north with him to the mountain resort of Baguio, where she had planned to spend her Easter vacation. In just a few days of hard persuasion he was able to convince her of the mutual value of their union, and on May 1, 1954, they were married by a justice of the peace in the little mountain town of Trinidad. From meeting to marriage, the whole affair took only 11 days.

The future first lady of the Philippines had been born on July 2, 1929, to Remedios Trinidad, the second wife of Vicente Orestes Romualdez. In the powerful first family of Leyte province, which boasted a number of senators, congressmen, and supreme court justices, Vicente Orestes turned out to be the family loser, and Remedios soon discovered that she had made a very bad marriage. Her antagonistic stepchildren, combined with a weak husband who took their side against hers, made Remedios's life so unbearable that she moved herself and her children into the garage near Vicente Orestes's house in Manila. Imelda watched her mother suffer for years until her death from pneumonia in 1937. After the death of Remedios, Vicente Orestes decided he could no longer afford the house in Manila and moved his entire family back to Leyte province. For the rest of his life, he would remain the poor Romualdez. For 10 years, financial trouble forced him to move his family from town to town, but he finally settled in Calle Real, in a Quonset hut, a type of cheap, prefabricated metal structure usually used for army barracks, of which Imelda was very ashamed. To live in the shadow of the rich Romualdez family, whose elegant mansion at Gran

Danieling Romualdez was Imelda's cousin and the speaker of the Philippine House of Representatives in 1954. The wealthy Romualdez family was the major political power in Leyte, and Marcos used his marriage to Imelda to draw support in the south, where he was weakest.

Twenty-year-old Imelda Romualdez submitted this photograph for the Miss Manila contest. A difficult early life in an impoverished branch of the Romualdez family left Imelda with a burning need for attention and success.

Capitán was known throughout the province, was an intolerable humiliation to Imelda, a quiet, sensitive girl.

While in high school, Imelda won a minor beauty contest, becoming the Rose of Tacloban. She graduated with above-average grades and attended St. Paul's College, where she earned a degree in education. Convinced that she was destined for greater things than the provincial life could offer, Imelda packed her suitcase and moved to Manila in 1952. She lived with her cousin Danieling, who began to introduce Imelda into the politically influential circles in which he traveled.

In her biography of Imelda Marcos, Philippine journalist Carmen Navarro Pedrosa suggests that growing up poor in a wealthy family marked Imelda with a deep social inferiority complex, and she spent the rest of her life overcompensating for it. It was her thirst for revenge, according to Pedrosa, that

Marcos's opponent in the 1965 election was incumbent president Diosdado Macapagal, shown here with Marcos in 1961. When Macapagal reneged on a promise not to run in 1965, Marcos switched political parties to oppose him.

motivated her throughout her remarkable and flamboyant career. She strove to destroy those elite elements of Philippine society — the powerful, monied, aristocratic families — that had rejected her as a child.

In the early years of her marriage to Marcos, Imelda did not have an official government position or any source of income, but she definitely earned her keep. Known as by far the most energetic woman in Philippine politics, she traversed the country wooing votes for Ferdinand's first senatorial campaign in 1959. She put her bounteous charm to use shaking hands, singing at campaign rallies, and cultivating relationships with the rich and the powerful.

In the Philippines, elections for the Senate are nationwide, not regional as in the United States. The influence of Imelda's family name, especially in the south, and her tireless campaigning added hundreds of thousands of votes to Ferdinand's tally. He won his Senate seat by a landslide.

It was during his campaign for president of the Senate in 1963 that Marcos was first publicly accused of accepting bribes. A wealthy American businessman was secretly investigated by Philippine officials on corruption and bribery charges. When investigators raided his offices they found a ledger listing the names of politicians who had been bribed for political favors. Among the names was that of Ferdinand Marcos. When questioned about the source of his personal wealth, Marcos claimed he had made lucrative real estate investments as a lawyer. When other congressmen admitted having accepted bribes, Marcos insisted he was innocent. He admitted to having received $2,000 from the man, but he produced a receipt to prove he had given the money back. When the receipt was found to be a forgery, the National Bureau of Investigation began an inquiry. The affair, however, was quickly hushed up. It seems that Marcos had made powerful friends during his years in the House. Despite the bribery scandal, he won the Senate presidency, and his limitless ambition soon drove him to seek the nation's highest office, president of the Philippines.

Supporters surround presidential candidate Marcos as he casts his ballot in 1965. Marcos spent $8 million on the election, reportedly even pawning Imelda's wedding ring to buy votes.

The Philippine political system was largely modeled on that of the United States. It operated on a two-party system, the major ones in the early 1960s being the Nationalist and Liberal parties. The Philippine parties, unlike their models in the United States, were defined less by a general party platform than by the views of their predominant members. Candidates dictated party ideology, and they often moved back and forth between the parties as it suited their interests.

For the 1965 presidential election, Marcos's party, the Liberals, had already nominated incumbent president Diosdado Macapagal. When he found this route blocked, Marcos had no qualms about switching loyalties. He joined the Nationalist party and sought its nomination instead.

The Nationalist convention was "based on the highest bidder," Bonner reports. Marcos, it was later learned, spent a whopping $8 million on the election. He even pawned Imelda's wedding and en-

Angry demonstrators burn an Uncle Sam effigy to protest the killing of Filipinos on one of the U.S. military bases in the Philippines in 1965. During the mid-1960s a growing wave of anti-U.S. feeling led Filipinos to agitate against the United States and its air and naval bases in the Philippines.

gagement rings in order to buy votes. One delegate recalls that Marcos "flung 100-peso notes around like confetti." For Marcos, it was an investment that would pay off many times over.

Imelda would later reveal to U.S. assistant secretary of state for East Asia William Bundy that the secret of winning the nomination was their control of the staff of the convention center and the Manila Hotel, where the delegates stayed. "We had the bellhops; we had the waiters; we had the elevator boys; we had the desk clerks"; but the most important thing, according to Imelda, was that "we had the telephone operators, so the other side never got their calls."

With the party nomination secured, Marcos hit the campaign trail, promising voters around the country: "I will give you everything you want. Except my wife." But Imelda gave herself totally to securing votes for Marcos. She was an amazing campaigner, singing and enchanting crowds into states of envy, hope, and adoration. Some commentators said she was worth a million votes to her husband in the 1965 election alone.

Philippine elections are notorious for their preballot mudslinging as well as for blatant fraud. But in the 1965 presidential election, even the U.S. embassy, which generally looked the other way, was impressed by the dirt flung by the candidates. In one report, embassy officials called this campaign "a year-long propaganda orgy." President Macapagal and the Liberal party accused Marcos of all kinds of crimes: cheating peasants out of their land, padding his senatorial payroll, issuing bad checks, and filing fraudulent war damage claims. (Although Marcos's fraudulent claim for medals was not yet revealed, it was known that he had made claims for property damage done during the war that were rejected by Washington.) The Liberal party's assault on Marcos was so brutal, the *Far Eastern Economic Review* reported, that "few are willing to believe that anyone can possibly be so bad."

Indeed, at the time it was hard for anyone to believe Marcos was as corrupt as his critics main-

tained. He had engineered for himself a spotless image: brilliant lawyer, war hero, patriot. He was so righteous in his anticorruption rhetoric; his battle cry for the campaign was *Walang Palakasan*, which can be translated as "no weight throwing," "no favors given," or "no name-dropping." If elected president, he promised to rid the government of the insidious corruption that had lined the pockets of the rich while increasing the misery of the poor for so many years. Young, attractive, energetic, and charismatic, Ferdinand and Imelda were compared to John and Jacqueline Kennedy, the beloved late president and former first lady of the United States. Voicing the same sort of hopeful, patriotic ideas that John Kennedy had in his 1961 election campaign, Marcos captured the imagination and aspirations of the Filipinos.

A typical village of the Moros, or Muslims, who live in the southern Philippines, one of the most depressed areas of the country. In his presidential campaign, Marcos promised government programs to improve conditions in the countryside.

Newly elected president Marcos and his family acknowledge the cheers of the crowd, December 1965. Many Filipinos and foreigners alike were optimistic about Marcos's election, comparing the young, energetic leader to the late U.S. president John F. Kennedy.

Despite Marcos's fine rhetoric, the traditional Philippine election practices occurred. Votes were bought, stolen, and deliberately miscounted on both sides. But Marcos and the Nationalist party had a special flair for charm, not to mention a talent for deception and manipulation, and he won the election by a margin of more than 670,000 votes.

"Every form of waste, or conspicuous consumption and extravagance, shall be condemned as inimical to public welfare," Marcos promised. It is a tragic irony that within a decade he and Imelda would reach levels of vulgar consumption almost unknown to the modern world. It is not an accidental irony, however: Marcos used his "war against government corruption" as a smoke screen behind which he and Imelda could build their fortunes on the backs of the Philippine people. Marcos's finesse at saying one thing with apparent candor and earnestness, while intending and pursuing the exact opposite, made him the Philippine politician par excellence.

The first years of Marcos's rule were viewed with cautious optimism by both Filipinos and foreign interests. The new president had inherited a host of problems from his predecessor and had made a great many promises about solving them. In accordance with his campaign pledge to make the nation a great economic force, Marcos went to work building roads, schools, bridges, airports, and other projects. As he had promised, there was some economic growth during this period. But the money invested in his projects was borrowed from abroad at a high rate of interest, which eventually would burden the Philippines with a huge debt.

In foreign policy, Marcos made efforts to cement good relations with the United States, the source of most of the Philippine aid. In 1966 he pressed the Philippine congress for funding to send 2,000 non-combat troops to Vietnam, where the United States was rapidly becoming bogged down in a war. Although only a token gesture in terms of manpower, the move was a signal to the United States that the new Philippine president was ready to serve U.S. interests in the south Pacific. At the same time, Marcos maneuvered himself into a respectable position in the eyes of his neighbors, especially Malaysia, the island nation to the southwest. Border disputes between the Philippines and Malaysia had led to a rift between the two countries. Marcos opened talks with the Malaysians, thus restoring formal relations. He also fostered a good image with the Japanese, another potential lucrative source of aid and investment in the Philippines.

In order to increase revenue, Marcos announced that his government would crack down on smuggling and corruption in the Philippine customs service and improve the collection of taxes in the countryside. He instituted an agricultural production and distribution program to enable the Philippines to feed itself without grain imports. (In 1968 the Philippines did achieve temporary self-sufficiency in rice production.) He began work on land reform to help the tenant farmers in the countryside, who worked the enormous plantations as virtual serfs. Agricultural reform had been one of the

He [Marcos] would never move until he was very, very sure. So long as he could use you, . . . he would use you. He'd embrace you like a cobra. He was a sneaky bastard. He was not an open man, but he was cunning. He was brilliant and he knew how to use power.
—BENIGNO AQUINO
on the political skills
of Marcos

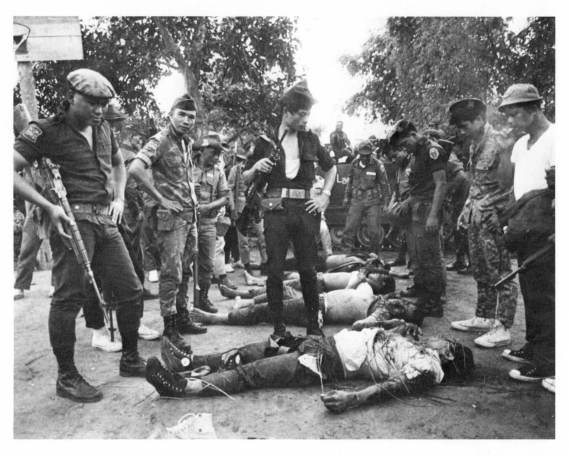

Four Huk rebels lie dead after a skirmish with government troops. The Huks had been reconstituted as a communist guerrilla movement, demanding land reform and economic improvement. From the beginning of his presidency Marcos maintained a hard line against the communists.

most important issues facing all the Philippine presidents. It had been dissatisfied peasant farmers who largely made up the Huks; social unrest caused by the grossly unequal economic system was always a major destabilizing force in the country.

The early spirit of optimism about Marcos's presidency, however, gradually gave way to doubts and pessimism. Although some programs continued, including plans for increased agricultural production, the introduction of cash crops new to certain areas, such as tobacco and onions in Ilocos, and massive construction projects, both urban and rural, others never got off the ground or were hampered by inefficient or corrupt officials.

Indeed, the national revitalization program soon was derailed by corruption. Friends and political allies of Marcos began to make fortunes in the major construction projects. Contracts were given to Marcos men, who charged far more than the jobs were worth. Marcos got a kickback, the contractors took a huge cut, and the Philippine people sank deeper into poverty. Nevertheless, thanks to increasing amounts of U.S. aid, enormous foreign loans, and financial stimulation caused by the Vietnam War, the Philippine economy was stable in Marcos's first years as president.

In his new position, Marcos found a whole new world of opportunities to make money and consolidate his power. He took charge of the allocation of the millions of dollars in foreign aid and loans from the World Bank and the International Monetary Fund, organizations established to help third-world and developing nations. Marcos also pruned jobs from the Philippine government bureaucracy, as he promised he would, but the people he cut were soon replaced with officials loyal to him.

When Marcos became president he declared that his assets amounted to $30,000. His salary as president was equal to $5,600. However, a profile done on Marcos by the U.S. Central Intelligence Agency in 1969 concluded that Marcos had already accumulated several million dollars. Few people at the time thought to ask from where all this money had come.

6
Debt of Gratitude

Marcos had a master's eye for what future advantages could be gained by doing favors in the present. Early in his career he was able to gain the support of powerful figures, both in the Philippines and around the world, by doing favors for them and incurring their gratitude. For this, he expected something substantial in return.

There is an expression in the Philippines for this granting of reciprocal favors: *utang na loob*, which can be roughly translated from Tagalog as "debt of gratitude." *Utang na loob* is essential to understanding all politics in the Philippines, for it is deeply rooted in traditional Filipino relationships, both personal and professional. Marcos took the principle to an extreme by extending the limits of *utang na loob* first to the entire Philippine nation and then to the international community. Once he did favors for others, he expected support in return. Perhaps the most important people whose debt of gratitude he incurred were the five U.S. presidents from Lyndon B. Johnson to Ronald Reagan who backed him in exchange for his protection of American business and military interests in the Philippines.

The Marcoses took care of family and friends, divvying up the economy, from coconuts to casinos, and giving a piece to this relative, that friend. . . . Rarely, if ever, in history have so few stolen from so many.
—RAYMOND BONNER
American journalist

President Marcos plays a round of golf at a country club in the northern Philippine resort town of Baguio. By the time of his second term of office, Marcos was siphoning off huge amounts of money from the government and the economy to enrich himself and his family.

Marcos says good-bye to U.S. president Richard Nixon before the latter's departure from Manila, 1969. During his rule, Marcos kept the support of five U.S. presidents by protecting U.S. military and business interests in the Philippines.

Using *utang na loob*, Marcos recruited allies from below as well. It is said that he had at least 20,000 godchildren: Parents would name him godfather, expecting gifts and favors, and in return, they gave Marcos political support. Marcos kept a full-time staff of 20 to keep track of his godchildren and buy them birthday presents.

Marcos could not persuade or bribe everyone, though. Toward the end of his first term in office, there were rumblings of discontent, especially among the tenant farmers who kept awaiting the more equitable land redistribution promised by Marcos and among students who opposed the increasing Philippine dependence on the United States. The Huk movement in the countryside had degenerated into roving bands that began to clash more frequently with government troops. Students demonstrated against government corruption, and labor strikes erupted in the major cities. By the end of his term, in 1969, Marcos's popularity had dropped substantially.

Given his ambition and hunger for power, there was no question that Marcos would run for a second term, even though not one of the five presidents preceding him had been reelected. Perhaps this was partly because candidates felt required to make outrageous promises that could never be honored in the struggling country. Disappointed, the voters rejected the incumbent president in favor of the promises of the next candidate.

To get around this problem, Marcos simply bought the election. The previous one, in 1965, had been seen by many as the country's most corrupt, but the 1969 election far surpassed it. Marcos is said to have spent about $50 million on his reelection campaign, $16 million more than U.S. president Richard Nixon had spent on his own campaign the year before.

On the surface, Marcos's campaign against Liberal party candidate Sergio Osmeña stressed his administration's achievements in road building, housing, education, and food production. He promised expanded social services, greater industrialization, more effective law enforcement, and a streamlined bureaucracy. Imelda also played her part in the 1969 campaign. She traveled around the country giving speeches, singing to the people, and pointing out how far the Philippines had already come under Ferdinand Marcos.

But below the surface, the campaign was not so benign. It relied on what are known in the Philippines as "the three g's" — goons, guns, and gold — to keep Marcos in office. His supporters even integrated convicted criminals into the Constabulary (the Philippine national police) to help intimidate voters and alter results. The elections were the most violent the nation had known. When the ballots were finally counted, Marcos had beaten Osmeña by almost 2 million votes out of 9 million cast.

Though Marcos was already a rich man by the time of the 1969 elections, he did not use his own money to buy the election. In a variety of devious ways, Marcos diverted government funds into his own campaign coffers. Some currency that had been taken out of circulation and was supposed to be destroyed was used by Marcos to buy votes. The resulting oversupply of money in the economy contributed to the financial decline in succeeding years and the drastic devaluation of the Philippine peso.

Liberal party candidate Sergio Osmeña opposed Marcos in the presidential election of 1969. Marcos's early popularity had quickly degenerated, and to avoid losing in 1969, he bought the election, one of the most violent the nation had then seen.

Marcos's inauguration for his second term was held in January 1970. In his speech, Marcos promised, "I will not demand more of you than I demand of myself and the government — neither wealth nor power shall purchase privilege." Upon emerging from the inaugural hall, the president and first lady were met by a barrage of stones and bottles lobbed by a crowd of about 20,000 disgusted students and workers. A few days after the inauguration, intense rioting rocked Manila. Outside Malacañang Palace, a day-long demonstration began with a march and ended with a mock trial of the Marcoses and the United States, both of whom were found guilty. Even at this stage, the United States was so intimately linked with Marcos in the minds of Filipinos that the U.S. government was denounced for the election abuses as well. Filipinos believed that the United States must have known about the fraud but still supported Marcos. The U.S. embassy was pelted with rocks and homemade firebombs as demonstrators shouted "Imperialist Pigs!" and "Yankee, Go Home!" The riot became known as the First Quarter Storm because of the strong student involvement. The disturbances continued until April 1970.

Marcos blamed the worsening national crisis on his critics, saying that they had stymied economic development by sowing rumors to drive away investors; prevented social services from reaching the people; encouraged strikes to produce an artificial scarcity of food, consumer goods, and exports; undermined the faith of the people in their public officials; and used sex, drugs, and pornography to destroy the moral fiber of the youth.

The president blamed the rioting on communist subversives. However, a U.S. State Department secret study analyzing the radical movements concluded that the riots in the Philippines were not based in communist ideology but were reactions to unbearable economic and social conditions. Raymond Bonner writes that in the "desperately impoverished" Philippines, "more than half the country's children under the age of ten suffered from malnutrition. . . . Only one of every ten chil-

> *Politics galvanizes into action all the beautiful hopes that a man can nurture in his heart for his country and for his nation. Politics is my life.*
> —FERDINAND MARCOS

64

dren was normal; the rest were seriously retarded because of poor diet."

In response to a growing sense of nationalism and a desire to restore some stability, a constitutional convention began sessions in the summer of 1971. There had long been a demand for revision of the 1935 constitution, which had been overseen by the United States and which was felt by many to be too economically favorable to the Philippines' former colonial master. Special elections were held to select the delegates to the 1971 convention, but shortly after the convention began, it became clear that President Marcos was not going to let the delegates decide the issues on their own. On the contrary, Marcos hoped to alter the constitution so as to protect his own career. Most important, he needed to persuade the convention to extend the current limit of two presidential terms. If the convention failed to

First lady Imelda Marcos casts her vote in the 1971 special election for delegates to the constitutional convention. Imelda campaigned tirelessly for the candidates who would support Marcos's interests at the convention.

By the early 1970s, Liberal party leader Senator Benigno S. Aquino emerged as the man most likely to challenge Marcos in the 1973 presidential election. Although Philippine presidents could by law serve only two terms, Aquino feared that Marcos would refuse to relinquish power.

make that change Marcos would be forced out of the presidency in 1973, when his second term was up. Documented cases came to light of bribery, harassment, and blackmail of delegates by Marcos forces. But many delegates held out, even against these pressures. In addition, opposition figures were agitating to include a provision that not only forbade Marcos from seeking a third term, but also prohibited Imelda from succeeding him.

Marcos was concerned over his loss of popularity because congressional elections were scheduled for 1971, and the Liberals were rapidly gaining support. On the evening of August 21, 1971, at Plaza Miranda in downtown Manila, the Liberal party held a rally to announce its slate of candidates. Suddenly, two hand grenades were tossed onto the temporary platform where many of the candidates were standing. At the same time, explosives went off underneath it. The Plaza Miranda bombing claimed the lives of 10 people and wounded about 100, including the candidates for mayor, vice-mayor, and several councilors of Manila. All eight senatorial candidates, including Sergio Osmeña and the leading candidate, veteran politician Jovito Salongo, were seriously wounded. Some were maimed for life.

Marcos immediately blamed the communists and suspended habeas corpus, the right of an accused to a fair and speedy trial. (The danger of suspending habeas corpus is that a citizen can be held in detention on unknown charges for an indefinite period of time.) He then charged the Liberal party leader, Senator Benigno Aquino, who had been attending a dinner party at the time of the attack, of collusion with the communists. Although the perpetrators of the bombing have never been caught, U.S. intelligence sources were convinced at the time that the Marcos military was behind it. It remains unknown what role, if any, Marcos himself played in the attack. In any event, the Plaza Miranda bombing served Marcos's purposes by increasing tension in the capital.

If Marcos forces were behind the bombing, they created a backlash against the president when sympathy for the injured Liberal candidates resulted in an overwhelming Liberal victory in the congressional elections. Marcos did not expect the defeat, and he was not the type to leave his future in the hands either of chance or the capricious will of the people. He set to work on the final touches of an alternate plan, one that he had considered before: the implementation of martial law. Martial law, intended for times of national emergency, meant that normal government procedures would be suspended and the president would assume all powers. But for such a drastic step, Marcos would need justification in the eyes of the world, especially in the United States, on which Marcos was critically dependent. It was time to call in his debt of gratitude from the United States.

Marcos knew that leaders in the United States and among his other allies would accept the most abhorrent actions as long as they were carried out in the name of anticommunism. He knew the United States had sanctioned, even at times engineered, the overthrow of third-world governments in the name of fighting communism. Marcos proceeded to exaggerate wildly the extent to which the small

Marcos talks with Bernabe Buscayno, captured leader of the outlawed Communist party of the Philippines, founded in 1968. Buscayno, commonly known as Commander Dante, helped form the military arm of the communists, the New People's Army (NPA), which pledged to overthrow Marcos.

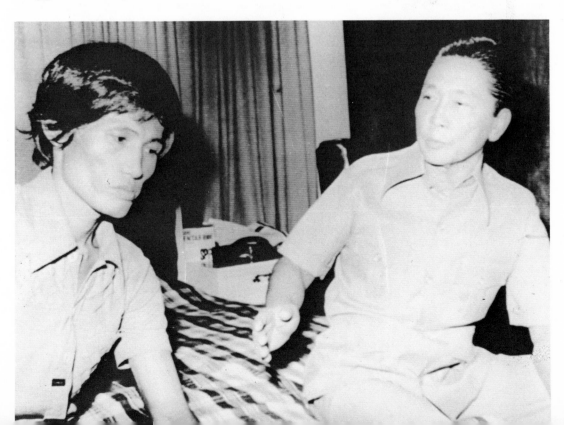

Secretary of Defense Juan Ponce Enrile reviews a naval honor guard in Manila in 1970. Enrile was one of Marcos's strongest supporters and provided the military backing the president used to maintain his power.

armed communist movement in the Philippines posed a threat to his government and, just as importantly, to U.S. interests in the Philippines.

The old Philippine Communist party had been largely broken up in the 1950s with the defeat of the Huk movement. In December 1968 Bernabe Buscayno, known as Commander Dante, and a group of university students formed a new Communist party of the Philippines (CPP) and established as its military arm the New People's Army (NPA). Maoist in ideology, the CPP pledged to foment revolution in the countryside and to rally the peasants, as Mao Zedong had done in China in the late 1940s, in order to overthrow the wealthy and occupy the land that they felt rightfully belonged to the people. The NPA found some strong support in pockets of central and northeast Luzon province, but generally, recruitment was slow.

Marcos cited the threat of the New People's Army as a primary reason for the declaration of martial law. According to Bonner, the president claimed there were at least 8,000 armed NPA members with

10,000 active supporters and perhaps 100,000 sympathizers. However, at the time martial law was declared, the threat posed by the communists was minimal. A U.S. State Department Bureau of Intelligence and Research study pointed out, "Its [the NPA's] military operations were at a low level and confined to remote areas." Another intelligence report put the total number of military and support members at 9,000. The Rand Corporation, a conservative U.S. research institution, estimated that there were only 1,000 NPA guerrillas. Later, in its own history, the NPA stated that at the time martial law was declared in 1972 it had had only 350 men with rifles.

In addition to simply exaggerating the numbers of armed guerrillas, Marcos distorted the threat by staging demonstrations and bombings and attributing these to the communists. As the constitutional convention continued to debate through early and mid-1972 without satisfying Marcos's needs, rumors flew that Marcos was planning to seize power. (Marcos's defense minister, Juan Ponce Enrile, after his defection in 1986, admitted that many of the bombings that took place before the martial law declaration were engineered by Marcos.)

The U.S. naval base at Subic Bay is an extremely important installation for U.S. interests in the South Pacific. During the early 1970s Philippine nationalists began calling for the removal of the Subic Bay base and of Clark Air Base in order to preserve Philippine integrity and self-sufficiency.

Along with Marcos, the economic elite was being threatened by the increasingly liberal tenor of popular opposition politics. The peasants were clamoring for true land reform and the redistribution of the great wealth that was firmly in the hands of a few: It was estimated that 5 percent of the population controlled 95 percent of the wealth.

The United States was also feeling the heat. The U.S. military installations in the Philippines — Subic Bay Naval Base and Clark Air Base — were two of the largest and most important stations outside the continental United States. Philippine nationalists, gaining more and more popular support, were calling for the removal of the bases on the grounds that the cost of their presence, in terms of national independence and integrity, was greater than the benefits reaped in the form of U.S. aid.

The United States had grown to depend on its privileged economic relationship with the Philippines, making an average profit of $3.58 for every dollar invested between 1946 and 1974. Of this amount, $2 went back to the United States. This represented billions made in the Philippines for the American economy. In August 1972 the Philippine

Members of a farming family sit down for a meal. As the Marcoses grew richer, most Filipinos fell deeper into poverty. At one point only 5 percent of the population controlled 95 percent of the nation's wealth.

A month after the declaration of martial law, passersby read a government directive to surrender weapons and observe the curfew. Marcos imposed martial law in September 1972 after receiving assurances from U.S. president Nixon that no action would be taken against him.

congress showed its decreasing tolerance for American interests when it made two rulings that damaged U.S. business interests. The United States did not want to see its status jeopardized any further by leftist or nationalist sentiment.

By early September 1972 the list of places in Manila hit by bomb blasts had grown: telephone offices, department stores, government buildings, the Philippine Sugar Institute, even, on September 5, Manila City Hall. The attacks caused power blackouts and water main disruptions. The opposition continued to blame Marcos for the bombings. Evidence of the president's intentions came with the astonishing announcement by Senator Aquino to the Philippine Senate on September 13 that Marcos planned to impose martial law in Manila. Aquino had laid his hands on the government plan, called Operation Sagittarius, that provided the details for the act. Marcos was forced to admit that a plan for martial law existed but said he had no intention of using it.

Aquino's discovery of the operation, however, pressed Marcos and his men to put the finishing touches on the plan. All that Marcos needed now was confirmation that he could use it without suffering negative consequences. He informed U.S. president Richard Nixon of the plan and learned that the United States would not do anything to stop him. Democracy in the Philippines thus ended with a phone call to the United States — the very country that had been the inspiration for that democracy.

There are several reasons why Nixon looked the other way when Marcos declared martial law. It mattered little to Nixon that a democracy, albeit an imperfect one, was being replaced by an authoritarian dictatorship, as long as U.S. interests would be protected. Nixon was a staunch anticommunist and believed that the Philippines needed a strong leader to hold the growing unrest in check. On the wider stage, the U.S. president was not overly concerned with the Philippines because he had bigger issues on his hands: the war in Vietnam, unrest at home, and, especially, the debacle of the Watergate scandal, which would ultimately lead to his resignation. By the time Marcos declared martial law, Nixon was already authorizing secret payments to silence the men who had just been indicted for breaking into the Watergate office of the Democratic party. In

Members of the New People's Army prepare for an assault against Philippine army troops. Under martial law, the NPA attracted thousands of poor Filipinos who despaired of any change under Marcos.

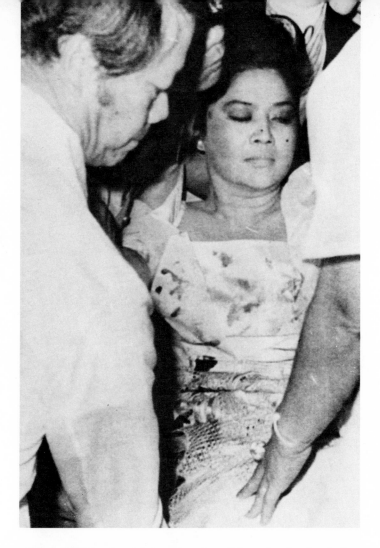

Imelda Marcos is placed on a stretcher after an assassination attempt at an awards ceremony in 1972. Her attacker, armed with a bolo knife, wounded her in the hands and arms before being gunned down.

short, Nixon had his own troubles; he looked the other way, and Marcos took this as a sign of consent.

For dramatic effect, Marcos and his wily minister of defense, Juan Ponce Enrile, staged an ambush on Enrile's motorcade. On September 22, 1972, as it was leaving the Wack Wack Golf Course, Enrile's blue Ford was riddled with bullets that shattered the rear window and laced the passenger door with holes. In what was heralded as a miracle at the time, though, the minister was riding in a security vehicle a few yards behind his own car and was not even scratched. Marcos blamed the attack on communists. At 9:00 that same evening, Marcos signed Proclamation 1081, the order implementing martial law, and a new era of repression and hardship for Filipinos began.

7
The New Society

Marcos's first action under the new law, which suspended habeas corpus and gave him nearly unlimited personal powers, was to arrest Senator Benigno S. Aquino, his most outspoken political opponent. Aquino, who many thought was going to be elected president in 1973 and was the person most likely to rally opposition to Marcos's decree, was picked up shortly after midnight. Other leading opposition politicians, including José Diokno and Ramon Mitra, were picked up before dawn.

By sunrise the next morning, the military had arrested scores of local politicians, priests, journalists, labor leaders, and others who were capable of organizing opposition to martial law. Newspaper presses, already rolling out Saturday's papers, were brought to a halt. Television and radio stations were closed down, and a curfew was imposed to keep potential troublemakers off the streets at night. Basic civil liberties, such as freedom of speech and assembly, were suspended. Restrictions on travel outside the country were instituted.

What he [Marcos] is clearly doing is erecting a one-man constitutional regime which permits him to stay in office indefinitely, with almost unlimited powers, under a veneer of parliamentary democracy.
—EDWIN L. BARBER III
former Foreign Service officer, shortly after Marcos declared martial law

Manila children of the barrio gather for a photograph beneath a calendar featuring a portrait of Imelda. In her quest to beautify the capital city to attract tourists, Imelda erected new houses around the fringes of the slums to mask the squalor.

Imprisoned senator José Diokno (right) plays chess with one of his guards in 1972. After he declared martial law, Marcos arrested not only political figures but also students, reporters, labor leaders, and any others who might voice opposition to his new regime.

More than 8,000 people were arrested for political reasons in the weeks following September 22. Among those detained were congressmen, delegates to the constitutional convention, students, reporters, editors, and governors. Very few of them were communists advocating violent overthrow of the government. Most were expressing their opposition to Marcos in democratic ways. But to Marcos, addicted now to his power, they represented opposition to his plan to make the Philippines his own kingdom.

An eerie calm followed the declaration of martial law. Surprisingly, there was no sign of panic. The Associated Press reported at the time that "Filipinos appear to have accepted Ferdinand Marcos's declaration of martial law with the typical aplomb of a people always hoping for the best."

Marcos quickly and ruthlessly suppressed what little spontaneous resistance there was. Student demonstrations disappeared and church leaders were intimidated into silence. The business community initially viewed Marcos's promises of stability and economic recovery with relief. Balanced between fear and hope, the majority of people waited to see what Marcos would do next. Playing to the people's hopes, Marcos called the declaration of martial law a "democratic revolution" and distracted attention from the nature of the post–martial law regime by draping it in the rhetoric of social justice.

"Social justice is as fundamental as food, clothing, and shelter," Marcos said at the time, promising to deliver all four in a "New Society." Marcos's New Society was to be a complete overhaul of the old way of life in the Philippines. He resurrected the old promise of land reform — a reform that would fundamentally change the countryside by abolishing the grossly unequal economic system that favored the wealthy plantation owners. With economic justice, Marcos declared, would come political stability to lessen the threat of the communists.

Marcos stated that martial law was the best way to abolish the traditionally unfair economic, corrupt political, and unequal social systems, because government in the hands of one man would be more efficient; a single decree could accomplish what the Philippine congress would surely have debated for months.

In his inimitable reverse-speak, however, Marcos promised the restoration of democracy and then dismissed the elected legislature so he alone ruled the nation. He promised a new, independent national identity and then pandered to American leaders and businessmen more energetically than had any Philippine president before him. He promised economic recovery and led the nation deeper into debt and economic chaos. He promised social justice and proceeded to adopt repressive policies, including imprisonment without charge, torture, and murder, in order to consolidate his own power. He promised to distribute land to the poor and then stole what little land they had. He promised to squash the communist movement, but his oppressive rule and unfair economic policies fanned the flames of the insurgency, causing it to spread like a fire out of control.

Let no man invoke friendship or blood kinship to enrich himself or to enhance his position.
—FERDINAND MARCOS
after declaring martial law

The new constitution, begun before martial law, was ratified two months after the declaration, when many of the convention delegates were behind bars on Marcos's orders. Not surprisingly, the new document accommodated Marcos's plans, allowing him to rule by decree and giving him the option to disband the legislature if he found it necessary.

He suspended the National Assembly, canceled the 1973 presidential election, and declared the continuation of his rule by martial law. He claimed that martial law was not a military takeover, but a victory for democracy over the forces of chaos. It soon became obvious, however, that the regime's authority stemmed not from the will of the people, but from the force of the military. One of Marcos's first moves was to bolster this authority by expanding the army from 60,000 to 155,000 soldiers. He replaced senior officers with younger men, many of them Ilocanos, whose loyalty to him was unquestioned.

With the executive and legislative branches of government under his control, Marcos forced the Supreme Court justices to tender their resignations. He reappointed some and replaced others with justices more in step with his interests. Marcos made it clear that they were all beholden to him for their jobs.

Having succeeded in getting complete political and military control, Marcos turned his attention to consolidating his economic power. As dictator, Marcos had the authority to *nationalize* businesses and corporations, to make them the property of the state. Throughout the decade he engaged in fraud of the most blatant sort, seizing sugar production plants, pineapple plantations, coconut farms and their oil extraction plants, public utilities, railroads, airlines, casinos, and television and radio stations, making them "public property" for a time and then either keeping them himself or giving them to friends and allies, who were referred to as his cronies.

"Crony capitalism," as the economic system during martial law came to be called, was not only unfair and illegal, it was also disastrous for the economy. Decisions were based not on their long-term economic merit, but on their immediate value to Marcos and his friends. By the mid-1970s, 7 out of 10 Filipinos were worse off as the result of martial law. For millions, the situation was desperate: Forty percent of the nation's deaths resulted from malnutrition; starvation was common in the depressed parts of the islands (particularly in the south); and millions were forced to live in shanty ghettos, scrounging for food, begging, or turning to crime or prostitution for income.

As most of the Philippines sank into economic misery, that part of the country accessible to the small group of very wealthy Marcos insiders was becoming more cosmopolitan and glamorous every day. The Marcoses were intent on turning the Philippines into a center of tourism to bring in more foreign money and to promote the Philippines throughout the world as a modern, progressive nation. International columnists poked fun at what they termed Imelda's "edifice complex," as the first

Imelda Marcos became a powerful political figure in her own right under martial law. She benefited from Marcos's control of the national economy and often used government funds to pay for shopping trips around the world.

The Philippine Cultural Center was one of Imelda's many building projects designed to glamorize Manila. The enormous glass and stone structure was erected on a landfill in Manila Bay.

lady oversaw the erection of building after building to improve the capital. But many people did not see the reverse side of Imelda's beautification campaign. The millions of dollars the Marcoses spent glamorizing Manila drained the treasury of money that could have been used to help the people who would never have a chance to step inside any of the dozen five-star hotels, some of which cost more than the annual budget of entire third-world nations.

Imelda's projects included the Philippine Cultural Center, a grand glass and stone edifice built on a landfill along Manila Bay; the luxurious Philippine Folk Arts Center, hurriedly built to host the 1974 Miss Universe pageant; the Philippine International Center, an enormous convention hall; and the Philippine Film Center, suggested by Imelda's good friend, Hollywood actor George Hamilton, and built so rapidly that several men died in construction accidents. Each one drained the besieged treasury of millions of dollars and benefited only the very rich Filipinos and foreign visitors.

Martial law brought a new calm to the streets, but it did not put an end to the political unrest or the social chaos of the pre–martial law years. In fact, by driving the left underground Marcos forced its members to organize themselves more carefully and efficiently and to adopt more radical tactics. Many students who formerly vented their opposition to Marcos in public rallies took up arms and joined the revolutionary NPA in the hills. Farmers in the countryside, forced into ever-deepening poverty, saw the NPA as the only way to survive. One NPA soldier declared, "Marcos is the best recruiter we have."

In order to counter the now illegal opposition to his rule, Marcos relied on counterinsurgency tactics that descended on the nation like a dark cloud of terror. Civilian arrests, torture, and murder became commonplace. In the countryside, where the NPA was making its most dramatic gains, government squads used terror tactics to suppress any dissent. People disappeared into places known as "safehouses" — remote, secluded buildings where screams could not be heard and torture could be carried out without fear of discovery. A process known as "salvaging" became commonplace under Marcos: The victim was kidnapped and murdered and the body disposed of so that the cause of death was unknown and indeterminable. Vocal opponents of the martial law regime found that the Marcos forces took revenge on their families, kidnapping and even murdering innocent people in order to silence an outspoken relative. Marcos saw people as either communists or his supporters. Many people who thought of themselves as neither often wound up in the communist camp, considering it the lesser of two evils.

Between 1972 and 1982 as many as 100,000 Filipinos were killed in the civil violence. Most of them were killed for political reasons or simply to frighten the people into silence and obedience. During that decade 65,000 were detained in military prisons and concentration camps, most of them for their political beliefs, denied the right to a hearing or trial.

The more repressive the Marcos regime became, the more difficult it was for the United States to justify its support of the dictator. President Jimmy Carter, for instance, distanced himself from Marcos in public, criticizing the Philippine president's

Cuban leader Fidel Castro conducts Imelda on a tour of a youth camp outside Havana in 1975. Imelda saw herself as the Philippines' greatest ambassador and reveled in the publicity of meeting important heads of state.

strong-arm tactics. Still, he felt he had no choice but to support Marcos generously with American money—U.S. interests were too valuable to risk by withdrawing support.

Marcos had always paid close attention to U.S. politics, and he understood it well. He knew that he would continue to get huge amounts of U.S. money (he received more than $2 billion over the dozen years of his dictatorship) and the political support of American presidents as long as he did three things: protect the security of the U.S. Navy and Air Force bases on the islands, portray the islands as one of the front lines in the struggle between communism and democracy, and protect the billions of U.S. dollars invested in the islands. American business interests in the Philippines involved such major corporations as Pepsi, General Electric, General Motors, and Proctor & Gamble, and Americans had invested heavily in Philippine industry, agriculture, and the export trade.

During the martial law years Imelda Marcos became a power in her own right. In 1975 Ferdinand appointed her governor of Metro Manila. (Metro Manila, created by decree, was an area of 4 cities and 13 towns clustered around the capital, Manila, and the administrative center, Quezon City.) She took this post as chief executive officer of one of the world's largest cities without any real political experience. But her wealth and power, and the fact of martial law, ensured that any public criticism of her appointment would be silenced.

Imelda was useful in Ferdinand's quest to woo foreign politicians and investors. Acting as an ambassador-at-large, she traveled the world over, winning the hearts of diplomats and statesmen. With her disarming charm, stunning beauty, and extravagant presents, she impressed such important American officials as Henry Kissinger, secretary of state under Richard Nixon, and Presidents Gerald Ford and Ronald Reagan. Imelda lived for publicity; even on minor issues, she would abruptly fly off to a country to meet with another leader — Fidel Castro of Cuba, Muammar Qaddafi of Libya, the Shah of Iran. With the imposition of martial law, she could travel as extravagantly and ostentatiously as she wanted, knowing that she could always censor it out of the Philippine media.

Imelda accompanies Mrs. Douglas MacArthur to a Philippines' cultural exhibit in New York. Imelda's extravagant world trips, on which she would bring an entire entourage of maids, friends, and reporters, fueled a deep resentment among Filipinos.

In December 1975 *Cosmopolitan* magazine published a story entitled "The Ten Richest Women in the World." Imelda Marcos's photograph appeared between those of Queen Elizabeth II of Britain and American actress Dina Merrill. The article suggested that Imelda might have even topped the list, but the true extent of her wealth was unknown. It was a remarkable statement, considering that neither Imelda nor Ferdinand had any inherited wealth, and his salary as president for the preceding 10 years was only $5,600 a year.

Imelda's government-sponsored junkets around the world, in which she would use one or sometimes two 747 jets to carry her baggage and her entourage of sycophants, became symbolic of the decadence under Marcos and martial law. The first lady had no qualms about having an entire department store closed to the public or opened after hours in order to shop alone, spending hundreds of thousands of dollars in a single spree. She bought up real estate, jewels, furs, antiques, fine art, and anything else that was expensive, in quantities that boggled the mind.

The years 1976 to 1980 saw an intensification in the mismanagement and corruption that riddled the Marcos government. The economy was largely in the hands of the Marcos and Romualdez families and their cronies. The repression grew worse as the torture of prisoners and the political killings continued, and the government kept a tight rein on all the media. The situation became so bad that Marcos drew the criticism of a powerful enemy: the Catholic church.

The Philippine church had for the most part been silent about martial law. Marcos did not control the church, which had an independent organization and financial base, and he did not want to antagonize its leaders. But under martial law, the country was descending into ruin so quickly that the church felt compelled to get involved. Jaime Cardinal Sin, the archbishop of Manila and the highest clerical official in the Philippines, announced a policy of "critical collaboration" with the regime, by which he meant that the church would not actively oppose the government but would speak out against any offenses it felt had to be addressed. The church started to document cases of torture and abuse and helped those who were driven into desperate poverty by the Marcos regime. With its own newspaper and radio station, it offered an alternative to the Marcos-run media.

The increasing criticism by the church encouraged other groups, especially the intellectuals, to become more vocal in their opposition, and by 1977 the anti-Marcos protests were attracting increased international attention. The following year, Marcos formed his own party, the *Kilusang Bagong Lipunan*, the New Society movement. KBL members, to no one's surprise, dominated both the assembly elections held in April 1978 and local elections held in 1980; both campaigns were marked by the fraud characteristic of elections under martial law. The political opposition stepped up its attacks against Marcos. In August 1980 eight groups drew up a declaration, entitled the National Covenant of Freedom, denouncing Marcos and martial law. Shortly afterward, the opposition formed a coalition group called the United Democratic Opposition (UNIDO).

Marcos responded to increasingly critical world opinion by announcing that he would end martial

Filipino students and workers stage a rally at the U.S. embassy in Manila to demand the removal of the U.S. bases in 1982. To the Filipinos, the United States's firm support of the Marcos regime made it as guilty as the dictator in the suppression of democracy in the Philippines.

In July 1983 Benigno Aquino spoke of his plans to return to the Philippines. After being imprisoned for seven years, Aquino was released in 1980 to undergo heart surgery in the United States. Afraid that civil war was looming for his country, he wanted to return to talk Marcos into stepping down.

law on January 1, 1981. Before formally ending it, however, he signed two decrees known as the "security code" and the "public order law" that constitutionalized most of his dictatorial powers and provided that the writ of habeas corpus remained suspended for people arrested for crimes involving state security — which were defined, of course, by the Marcos government.

The "lifting" of martial law was only a token gesture. Strikes and demonstrations were still illegal unless authorized. Publications were still illegal unless licensed by the State Media Council. And, though a parliament would be elected, it had little meaning because Marcos had constitutional amendment 6, which allowed him to make or overrule any law by simple decree. Although a great noise was made over the lifting of martial law, no one in the Philippines was fooled. Marcos remained a dictator.

By this time, Marcos's political nemesis, Benigno Aquino, was a free man. After spending seven and a half years in jail, an ailing Aquino was released because of international pressure placed on Marcos. Aquino, still widely viewed as the strongest opposition leader to Marcos and virtually idolized by his countrymen, was allowed to fly to the United States for heart surgery in May 1980. After his operation, Aquino remained in voluntary exile in the United States, teaching at Harvard and the Massachusetts Institute of Technology and continuing his outspoken denunciation of Marcos's martial law regime. As he heard the reports of the worsening situation in the Philippines, he feared that his country was headed for civil war. He decided to return to challenge Marcos himself.

In May 1983 Aquino received a visit from Imelda Marcos, who tried everything to keep Aquino from returning to the Philippines. She warned him that the secret service had uncovered leftist plots to assassinate him if he returned. She could not promise he would not be killed by activists on the right, either. When these veiled threats failed to dissuade him, she tried bribery, offering any amount of money he needed to set up a business in the United

States. Aquino knew he might be killed if he returned to the Philippines, but, he said, he had no choice. It was his last chance to alter the terrible crash course Marcos had imposed on the nation, and he could not let his homeland go to the devil without a fight.

On August 21, 1983, accompanied by journalists and friends, Aquino went back to the Philippines. He had kept his itinerary a secret, hoping to fool the Marcos intelligence sources, and flew to his native country from Taiwan. When his plane landed in Manila, soldiers came aboard and escorted Aquino down a stairway brought to the side of the plane. Shortly after Aquino left the plane, a single gunshot rang out, followed by a volley of shots. Aquino fell to the ground, a bullet in his head. Photographs of the scene show a dead man lying near Aquino. Marcos later claimed that this man, Rolando Galman, had shot Aquino and was immediately killed by the security soldiers present. Marcos also claimed that the lone gunman was a communist conspirator who had somehow made his way through the sea of military men sent to the airport to "protect" the former senator and got close enough to Aquino to kill him with a single bullet.

No one believed Marcos. Most Filipinos believed that Galman was no trained assassin, only another victim set up to take suspicion off the real killers. To the deeply religious people of the Philippines the return of Aquino had been seen as a redemption of sorts, a chance to shake off the corruption and decay of the Marcos regime. Their hope for the future of the Philippines had been tied to his return. Aquino's murder was followed by a moment of silence, of hopelessness; the people's messiah had been slain. However, that silence was followed by a sound that would change the lives of the Marcoses and alter the course of Philippine history — a roar of outrage.

> We must convince the President [Marcos] to bring democracy back. I'm appealing to him to grant me an interview. He is the only man who can return the Philippines to democracy peacefully. Otherwise, we're down the road of an El Salvador.
> —BENIGNO AQUINO
> on the day of his death

8

The Fall

Thousands of people thronged outside the small Aquino home on Times Street in Manila. At the front door the crowd converged into a single stream. From the poorest street beggars to the richest businessmen, they viewed the body of Benigno Aquino. The coroner had not retouched the bullet hole in Aquino's head or the bruises on his face. The victim's clothes were still stained with his blood. Aquino's mother had instructed that Benigno's body be left as he had fallen, so everyone could see what Marcos had done to her son. The nation mourned the slaying of its last democratic hope, and the Filipino people, pushed beyond the point of fear, took to the streets.

There are many theories about who planned the assassination and how much Marcos actually knew. Virtually no one believed the president's story that a lone communist killed Aquino. On the other hand, it was also difficult to believe that Marcos was behind the clumsy murder. He was too shrewd a politician to ignite the opposition and turn world opinion against himself by killing Aquino in such an obvious way, analysts said.

> While a dictator like Marcos might serve short-term U.S. interests, he will more often than not be antithetical to America's long-term interests, as Marcos was to demonstrate. . . . The Communists had become a threat to the Philippines, the economy had been destroyed, and the army had been corrupted and demoralized.
> —RAYMOND BONNER
> American journalist

Marcos and U.S. president Ronald Reagan watch White House ceremonies in October 1982. Reagan was a staunch supporter and ideological ally of Marcos but was forced by political realities to withdraw his backing after the 1986 election, which led to the dictator's downfall.

Jaime Cardinal Sin, the archbishop of Manila, prays over the body of Benigno Aquino. The popular opposition leader was assassinated immediately upon his return to the Philippines in August 1983.

Moreover Marcos, who was suffering from systemic lupus erythematosus, a disease that slowly destroys the internal organs, had a kidney transplant only days before the assassination and was still recovering when the murder took place. A palace insider later said that when Imelda walked into Ferdinand's office just after the news of the killing was out, Ferdinand was so furious he threw something, hitting Imelda just below the eye. As the bruise swelled, Imelda threw a tantrum, throwing thousands of dollars worth of antiques against walls and smashing them on the floor. This episode seems to support what many diplomats and intelligence officers believed: Imelda and her brother Benjamin planned the assassination while Marcos was out of commission, and Marcos, who recognized the seriousness of the blunder, was furious.

Whoever was responsible for Aquino's death, a political fire had been set. It spread so fast during the months following the assassination that many experts believed the drama would end with a full-scale civil war. In such a case, analysts felt, the United States would find itself right in the middle, supporting an unpopular dictator against a popular opposition that, linking the United States to the hated ruler, was growing increasingly hostile to U.S.

interests. For the first time since martial law had been declared in 1972, the people defied the government prohibitions on demonstrations and gathered in the streets by the thousands to denounce Marcos and his regime and demand change.

Fanning the flames of social unrest, the economy took a sharp dip after the assassination. Foreign investors, fearing the growing instability in the country, stopped bringing in money and began to withdraw what they had in the islands. Even Filipino businessmen began to take their money out of the country and salt it away abroad.

The Marcoses and their business cronies continued to make money, however. Perhaps sensing that their racket was coming to an end, they began desperately grabbing funds wherever they could get them. A World Bank report released in September 1984 stated that at least $3.1 billion of foreign loan money failed to reach its intended beneficiaries in the Philippines. In a case typical of the way in which funds were diverted, employees at the U.S. Agency for International Development discovered that Philippine government officials had taken $18 million in grant money intended to secure schools against

Anti-Marcos demonstrators march to Malacañang Palace holding pictures of people killed by government soldiers. Although no precise figures are available, the war that Marcos waged against his own people, which included kidnapping, torture, and murder, destroyed thousands of lives.

Ragpickers search through a mountain of garbage in an urban shantytown. More than any other group, the Filipino poor suffered miserably under Marcos, bearing the brunt of corruption and a failing economy.

typhoons and instead had invested it in a bank account in their own names.

The U.S. State Department released a stern statement on the Aquino assassination, deploring the incident and demanding that the Philippine government find out who was responsible and prosecute them to the full extent of the law. Despite these harsh words, the Reagan administration not only continued to pour money into the Philippines but actually increased military and development aid in an attempt to bolster Marcos against the growing radical anti-U.S. opposition.

The Catholic church began to speak out more openly against Marcos and his oppressive regime. Cardinal Sin criticized Marcos in his speeches and regular Sunday sermons. His opposition was taken by more moderate groups as a sanction for them to stand up against the dictator. As the one institution in the country not under the direct control of Marcos, the church would play a profound role in the nonviolent ousting of the first family.

In the months following the Aquino assassination, Marcos began to find himself isolated from other traditional allies as well. Even members of the business community who had benefited from Marcos's favor under martial law began to have second thoughts about participating in his plundering when they realized that it would soon leave their nation in a state of economic ruin. Perhaps they also feared possible adverse reactions to their cooperation with the Marcos regime if the government fell.

As always in the Philippines, the poor bore the brunt of the failing economy. Unemployment and underemployment were at all-time highs, and those who were employed at all received wages that had years earlier lost pace with skyrocketing inflation. Farm workers toiled long, hard hours in the sun for less than a dollar a day. Others barely eked out a living hawking cigarettes, newspapers, or mangoes on the streets of Manila for pennies a day.

Thousands of other poor and disenchanted young people took up arms. Having given up hope for democratic change after the assassination of Aquino, they joined the NPA, which was recruiting new members faster than it could arm them. In the decade since Marcos had declared martial law the NPA had grown from a ragtag group of a few hundred ill-equipped soldiers to a well-disciplined and well-armed force of approximately 20,000 guerrillas in 1984. "Our choices were reduced to two, fighting or surrendering to starvation," one young NPA recruit said in 1983. In the countryside, the rebels helped the people who were displaced because of government projects or the expansion of plantations. They provided quasi-governmental services in the rural areas of most of the Philippine provinces, setting up courts, sometimes distributing simple medicines, and collecting taxes. They also began to wage successful strikes against the much better equipped military units of the government.

As the months passed, and U.S. president Reagan continued to support Marcos, the once moderate opposition began to join the radical leftists in chanting their favorite slogan: "Down with the U.S.-Marcos dictatorship." If the United States continued to back Marcos, many analysts feared, the armed opposition would continue to grow and would expel

The motorcade of presidential candidate Corazon Aquino and her running mate, Salvador Laurel, passes through a sea of hands in Talisay on Negros Island. Aquino, the widow of the late senator, announced her candidacy in late 1985.

both the dictator and the U.S. interests, as had happened in Iran and Nicaragua in 1979. In those countries, where the United States had also supported unpopular dictators, the American presence had been ousted along with the dictators at a tremendous cost to U.S. economic and military interests. But U.S. policymakers could see no viable option to supporting Marcos. The Philippine president had eliminated most of the moderate opposition politicians whom the United States might have considered acceptable replacements for him. If the United States withdrew its support entirely, there was no telling who would end up in power — maybe someone even worse than Marcos — or what would happen to the U.S. bases in the Philippines.

Aquino's assassination attracted hundreds of reporters to the Philippines, and as their reports were filed, the world was shocked by the devastating poverty, the political repression, the unbelievable corruption. At about this time, a series of articles was published in the San Jose, California, *Mercury News* about Marcos's hidden wealth. The stories linked the Marcoses to millions of dollars worth of real estate and business in the United States.

For security and health reasons, Marcos seldom ventured into public during this period, but when he did appear, he was unflappable. He believed that no matter what threats Congress made about cut-

A crowd of government loyalists carries Marcos during a rally for the 1986 election. As Marcos saw the increasing popularity of Aquino, who drew crowds of thousands, he began to offer money to people to attend his rallies.

ting aid to the Philippines, the United States could not afford to let him fall. He was still the primary protector of U.S. interests on the islands. He still enjoyed a close friendship and ideological alliance with Ronald Reagan, the most popular president the United States had had in 20 years.

By October 1985, however, even President Reagan began to see that something had to be done. He sent his close friend and adviser Senator Paul Laxalt to the Philippines to urge Marcos to hold "credible" elections in 1987. If he did, the United States would have time to cultivate other candidates among the moderate pro-U.S. opposition or to back Marcos. That way, if Marcos won, and the election was relatively fair, or at least appeared so, his credibility would be restored. If he lost, the United States would have an acceptable replacement to protect its interests.

Marcos surprised everyone by taking the American proposal one step further. He announced that he would hold a presidential election in February 1986 — in three months. Declaring a "snap" election, one held before the appointed time, was a typically shrewd Marcos move that caught the Philippine opposition by surprise; it was divided, had no clear leader, and was unprepared for major campaigning. Marcos's decision had been opposed by Imelda, his Philippine advisers, and even the U.S. State Department. However, announcement of the snap election hushed outside criticism of Marcos's regime and paved the way for an increase in U.S. aid, now that the president was proving his dedication to democracy.

Most analysts believed that, despite his unpopularity, Marcos would win the election. After all, the legal opposition had been whittled away over the martial law years to a fraction of what it had been. What remained was divided into small factions, none possessing the sort of party machinery it would take to defeat Marcos. Even if the opposition could unify behind a viable candidate and come up with money and an organization to promote the candidate, what would stop Marcos from winning by cheating, the way he always had before?

We love your adherence to democratic principle and to the democratic process.
—GEORGE BUSH
in a toast to Marcos
in 1981

A smiling Corazon Aquino casts her vote for president on February 7, 1986. Despite fears of election fraud and intimidation by the Marcos forces, Aquino was confident of victory.

The one thing no one expected was the return to the political scene of Marcos's archenemy Aquino in the form of his widow, Corazon, affectionately referred to simply as Cory. After the assassination of her husband, the self-described "mere housewife" began to give heartfelt, humble speeches at demonstrations and rallies. Her speeches struck chords in the people that no one else seemed able to touch. Cory Aquino seemed the polar opposite of Marcos: honest, politically naive, and unambitious. Like them, she was a victim; like them, she had suffered at the hands of the Marcos forces; and like them, she wanted a new direction for the Philippines. If Benigno's murder was the straw that broke the camel's back, Cory was the spark that could start the spilled straw burning.

There was only one problem. Aquino was not interested in politics, let alone in becoming a politician and battling the most seasoned and ruthless one in Asia. When she was approached by opposition leaders as a possible candidate, she deflected their overtures by saying she would only consider running if they were able to gather a million signatures in a petition of support for her candidacy.

She was shocked when it took them only two weeks to gather the signatures. A very religious woman, Aquino looked inward, praying for the guidance to make such a momentous decision. She later told Cardinal Sin that she heard the voice of her husband advising her to carry on his fight to save the Philippines. She prepared to run against Marcos.

Marcos had an immeasurable advantage over the Aquino campaign. He still controlled the media — central to the success of any election campaign — the courts, the commission in charge of elections, the military, and the national treasury. Indeed, Marcos printed and spent $500 million on the 1986 election and paid people to attend progovernment rallies, coverage of which took up a huge portion of every evening's news broadcasts on the government-controlled stations. Aquino's rallies, which were much larger and more lively, barely received mention.

Nonetheless, as each day passed, the country became more and more intoxicated with "Corymania." Yellow was Aquino's campaign color, and Manila became a yellow city as banners were hung from

A nun counts ballot boxes at a polling station in one of Manila's slums. To prevent Marcos from cheating, people across the country volunteered to help monitor the election. The Catholic church played a critical role in documenting the fraud by the Marcos forces.

windows, ribbons decorated street signs and car antennas, and all sorts of yellow objects enlivened the drab corners where the urban poor hawked their wares. From high fashion to street chic, yellow was the color to wear. It was the color of sunlight after a long dark storm, and, for many, the color of hope.

As the election date of February 7 neared, Marcos realized that he had misjudged Aquino's ability to rally the people behind her. In public he feigned calm and confidence. But he was ill and exhausted. His anxiety began to show through his steely smiles, and his usually persuasive baritone voice began to weaken and falter. His face was alternately drawn and swollen from the dialysis treatments required for his kidney disease. For the first time in his political career, he was losing control, and his composure began to crack.

If Marcos had been well, the cheating that took place before and during the election would probably have been less obvious and bumbling. But Marcos had surrounded himself with devoted aides, not especially intelligent or competent ones. Now that he was ill and unable to control everything himself, many tasks fell into the hands of these faithful but incompetent servants, and the world witnessed the

Demonstrators carrying a ballot box with effigies of Marcos and Reagan urge people not to vote in the 1986 election. Many Filipinos, convinced that no election under Marcos could be conducted fairly, supported the NPA-sponsored boycott.

most obviously corrupt and violent election in the history of the Philippines.

The delegation of official observers from the United States, headed by Republican senator Richard Lugar, was appalled by the troops and hired thugs who stole ballot boxes, intimidated voters, and did whatever they could to influence the voting in favor of Marcos. Many voters got to their polling places to find that someone had already voted for them. Others were shocked to find that long-dead relatives had apparently voted. Lugar estimated that 10 to 40 percent of the Philippine people — those the Marcos forces thought might support Aquino — had been illegally disenfranchised or had their names taken off the voter registration lists.

Two organizations monitored the election. The members of the official government group, the Commission on Elections (COMELEC), were appointed by Marcos. A citizens' election watch group, called

Imelda Marcos, an obsessive shopper, financed her habit with government revenues. The full extent of her shopping sprees became known to the public in 1986, when it was revealed that she had accumulated more than 2,500 pairs of shoes.

On February 22, 1986, Defense Minister Enrile (left), army chief of staff Lieutenant General Fidel Ramos (right), and their supporters defected from the Marcos military. They appealed for help to Cardinal Sin (center), who called on the Filipinos to back the rebels.

the National Citizens Movement for Free Elections (NAMFREL), was made up largely of volunteers who counted the election returns. According to NAMFREL, despite the government fraud, Aquino won so overwhelming a majority of the votes that even after all the cheating she still came out ahead. There was only one thing left for Marcos to do — steal the votes cast for Aquino.

On February 8, the day after the election, the official count slowed and then stopped. When the tabulation resumed a few hours later, Marcos had miraculously taken the lead. The vote stealing by the Marcos forces was revealed when several computer operators at COMELEC walked out in protest at the order to change the votes from Aquino to Marcos. Afraid for their lives, they took refuge in a Manila church and informed the international press corps of what had happened.

On February 14, the Catholic Bishops' Conference of the Philippines issued a statement declaring the election fraudulent and calling for nonviolent resistance. Virtually no one believed that Marcos had gained more votes than Aquino. Nonetheless, on February 15, the official count was released and Marcos was declared the duly elected president by the Marcos-controlled National Assembly. The announcement of Marcos's official victory was not heard with the kind of helpless disappointment that had marked fixed elections in the past, however. People were outraged, certainly, but also they remained hopeful, as though they knew the episode was not over.

There were moments of despair. Throughout the country, Aquino election workers were found mur-

Supporters of the rebels deliver supplies to the soldiers barricaded at Camp Aguinaldo, outside Manila. Thousands responded to Cardinal Sin's plea, forming a human shield between the rebels and the Marcos troops sent to attack them.

Ferdinand and Imelda Marcos make their last public appearance in the Philippines, on a balcony of the presidential palace, on February 25, 1986. Hours later and only minutes ahead of an invading mob, the Marcos family was removed from the palace by the U.S. military.

dered. Filipinos will remember for decades the sense of abandonment they felt at President Reagan's comments on the election. After Reagan read a perfunctory review of a report on the election fraud monitored by the U.S. observer delegation, he said, "Well, I think that we're concerned about the violence that was evident there and the possibility of fraud, although it could have been that all of that was occurring on both sides. . . ." One Filipino said later, "It was at this moment that the majority of Filipinos realized that Reagan was a friend of Marcos, not a friend of the Philippines." Aquino herself delivered a blistering retort to Reagan for his moral lapse and diplomatic error. "I wonder at the motives of a friend of democracy who chose to conspire with Mr. Marcos to cheat the Philippine people of their liberation," she said.

But Aquino concentrated her energy on sustaining the hopefulness of her followers and searching for the next step. At a huge rally in Manila, Aquino announced her victory and asked the crowd of 1 million to boycott businesses owned by Marcos and his cronies (including San Miguel beer, the Philippine favorite) and take whatever peaceful measures necessary to get Marcos to recognize the people's choice. The crowd cheered and vowed to observe the boycott. But many wondered if demonstrations and boycotts would be sufficient and feared that armed struggle might be the only effective approach. However, in the end, the catalyst for the Philippine revolution came from an unlikely source: the Philippine armed forces, the backbone of the Marcos regime.

On February 22, Marcos's intelligence agents reported that Defense Minister Juan Ponce Enrile, a longtime ally of the president's, had been scheming with reformist military officers to seize Malacañang Palace in a coup. When Enrile's own sources discovered that Marcos had learned of the plot, he, Deputy Chief of Staff General Fidel Ramos, and the reformist officers fled to Camp Aguinaldo, the headquarters of the defense ministry, on the outskirts of Manila. With their limited firepower and support they expected to be quickly overcome by Marcos, who had all the resources of the military at his command.

Enrile got in touch with Cardinal Sin, who delivered a message over the Catholic radio station, Veritas (the Latin word for truth), to the people to come out of their homes and surround Enrile and his defectors with a human barricade so that Marcos could not get to them. When Marcos's tanks arrived they met a wall of humanity barring the way to the defectors. On the front lines nuns offered prayers, flowers, and food to the befuddled marines. The government soldiers defied orders to shoot at the crowds.

Hour by hour Marcos's allies deserted him. Enrile declared that Aquino was the true victor in the elections. The world watched in amazement as Filipinos turned out in the thousands to protect the defec-

Joyful Filipinos celebrate the end of the Marcos regime by burning an official portrait of Imelda. Just after the Marcoses left, a rampaging mob stripped off the barbed wire surrounding Malacañang and tore through the palace, removing symbols of the hated dictator and his wife.

tors. Rebel bands attacked the government television stations. Even most of Marcos's military defected, leaving him to fend for himself in Malacañang Palace. The Marcos family and some friends and advisers huddled in their besieged home, separated from the hungry mob outside only by a barbed wire fence and the few palace guards who stayed.

On the evening of Monday, February 24, Marcos called his family together. Daughters Irene and Imee sat at the end of Marcos's bed and begged him, tears rolling down their cheeks, to give up and accept an offer of asylum in the United States, which had been extended by Reagan through Stephen Bosworth, the U.S. ambassador to the Philippines.

The family was still collected there at 3 A.M. when Marcos called Senator Laxalt, with whom he had enjoyed a friendly relationship. The Philippine president asked for a guarantee that if he accepted the asylum offer he would not be punished, and Laxalt assured him he would not be. He asked Laxalt if the United States would agree to help set up a power-sharing arrangement between himself and Aquino. Laxalt said he would have to ask President Reagan and they hung up.

Laxalt called Marcos back two and a half hours later with the news that Reagan had rejected the idea of power sharing. "Does the president want me to resign?" Marcos asked. Senator Laxalt said he could not speak for the president but he himself thought Marcos should "cut and cut clean." He told Marcos, "The time has come." After a long tense silence Laxalt asked Marcos if he was still on the line. "Yes," Marcos said in a quivering voice almost paralyzed by emotion. "I am so very, very disappointed."

On the morning of February 25, Corazon Aquino was sworn in as the president of the Philippines. Earlier, Marcos had called Enrile at the rebel camp

An official portrait of the Marcoses, commissioned by Imelda, depicts the family in a royal fashion. The Aquino government, maintaining that the Marcoses had stolen billions of dollars in assets, sued them for what it claimed rightfully belonged to the Philippine people.

in a last-ditch effort to strike a deal, but nothing came of it. At noon, Marcos held his own inauguration. Two thousand stalwart Marcos supporters were bussed past the crowds of Aquino supporters into Malacañang for a free chicken dinner and to witness Marcos's macabre ceremony. When Ferdinand and Imelda came onto the balcony above the audience the crowd began to chant "Martial law! Martial law!" Imelda stood next to Marcos looking alternately panicked and stoic. Marcos himself mustered up all the energy remaining in his sickly frame and delivered a fierce, defiant speech. Although the inauguration was to be broadcast on Channel 9, the only television station that remained in government hands, just before the ceremony began Channel 9 surrendered to rebel forces. The Filipinos did not see the bizarre event.

An ailing Marcos is helped onto Hawaiian soil by U.S. military personnel. The Marcoses settled comfortably into exile in Hawaii, from where, it is claimed, Marcos launched efforts to undermine and ultimately overthrow Aquino and return to rule the Philippines again.

Before 9:00 P.M. that night Marcos was plucked from his palace one step ahead of the mobs climbing the fences outside and flown in a U.S. helicopter to Clark Air Base. He tried to arrange to visit his home province of Ilocos before leaving the country, but Aquino refused to permit it, fearing that Marcos would have been able to secure himself among his Ilocano supporters and launch a war on her new government. Marcos, Imelda, their children, and several close friends were taken to Guam, then flown to Hawaii, where they would remain as guests of the U.S. government.

The Marcos family occupied a small estate in the exclusive Makiki Heights section of Honolulu that doubled as home and a law office for Marcos. The former dictator occupied his time trying to fend off the many lawsuits and criminal charges brought against him by the Aquino government, which tried to recover some of the estimated $10 billion the Marcoses had stashed in hidden properties, Swiss bank accounts, and a maze of other worldwide investments.

Almost overnight Marcos had been transformed from a feared and hated dictator to a pathetic and quirky old man. After he was deposed he repeatedly tried to regain his place in the Philippines, financing those troops still loyal to him to attempt coups against the popular Aquino government and scheming to sneak out of the United States and return home.

Despite overwhelming evidence to the contrary, Marcos remained convinced that the Philippine people still wanted him. "The biggest mistake I ever made," Marcos said in Hawaii, "was leaving Malacañang Palace. It is clear to me now that we could have stayed, fought, and won."

Further Reading

Bonner, Raymond. *Waltzing with a Dictator: The Marcoses and the Making of American Policy*. New York: Times Books, 1987.

Chua-Eoan, Howard. *Corazon Aquino*. New York: Chelsea House, 1988.

Fernando, Gilda Cordero. *We Live in the Philippines*. New York: Bookwright Press, 1986.

Firth, Robert H. *Philippine Invasion 1941–1942: A Matter of Time*. rev. ed. Walnut, CA: Firth, 1981.

Johnson, Bryan. *The Four Days of Courage*. New York: Free Press, 1987.

Komisar, Lucy. *Corazon Aquino: The Story of a Revolution*. New York: Braziller, 1987.

Lawson, Don. *Marcos and the Philippines*. New York: Franklin Watts, 1984.

McDougald, Charles C. *The Marcos File: Was He a Philippine Hero or Corrupt Tyrant?* San Francisco: San Francisco Publishers, 1987.

Mercado, Monina Allarey, ed. *People Power: The Philippine Revolution of 1986*. Manila: The James B. Reuter, S.J., Foundation, 1986.

Pedrosa, Carmen Navarro. *Imelda Marcos: The Rise and Fall of One of the World's Most Powerful Women*. New York: St. Martin's Press, 1987.

Poole, Fred, and Max Vanzi. *Revolution in the Philippines: The United States in a Hall of Cracked Mirrors*. New York: McGraw-Hill, 1984.

Rosenburg, David A. *Marcos and Martial Law in the Philippines*. Ithaca, NY: Cornell University Press, 1979.

Schirmer, Daniel B., and Stephen R. Shalom. *The Philippine Reader*. Boston: South End Press, 1987.

Spence, Hartzell. *Marcos of the Philippines*. Manila: World Publications, 1979.

Wernstedt, Frederick L., and Joseph E. Spencer. *Philippines Island World: A Physical, Cultural, and Regional Geography*. Berkeley: University of California Press, 1978.

Chronology

Sept. 11, 1917	Born Ferdinand Edralin Marcos in Ilocos Norte, the Philippines
1934	Begins law studies at the University of the Philippines, Manila
Nov. 1939	Earns highest national score ever on bar examination Convicted of murder of father's political rival
Oct. 12, 1940	Presents own case to Supreme Court and wins acquittal
Dec. 7, 1941	Japan attacks the Philippines
April–May 1942	Surrender of U.S.-Filipino troops; Marcos among those on the Bataan Death March
July 4, 1946	Philippines gains independence
1949	Marcos elected to House of Representatives
May 1954	Marries Imelda Romualdez
1959	Elected to Senate; serves for five years
Nov. 30, 1965	Elected president of the Philippines
Nov. 1969	Reelected despite charges of widespread fraud
Aug. 21, 1970	Plaza Miranda bombing nearly destroys opposition
Sept. 21, 1972	Marcos imposes martial law; announces inauguration of his New Society
1972–1981	Maintains power through army terrorism, torture, and murder; Marcoses and cronies control national economy
Jan. 17, 1981	Marcos lifts martial law but retains dictatorial powers
Aug. 21, 1981	Opposition leader Benigno Aquino assassinated in Manila; anti-Marcos demonstrations erupt
Oct. 1985	Marcos announces snap election
Dec. 3, 1985	Corazon Aquino declares candidacy
Feb. 7, 1986	Election Day; Marcos forces charged with election fraud and violence
Feb. 15, 1986	National Assembly declares Marcos winner
Feb. 22, 1986	Defection of Defense Minister Juan Ponce Enrile and supporters; people rally to protect them from Marcos military forces
Feb. 24, 1986	United States withdraws support of Marcos
Feb. 25, 1986	Marcos and family leave for exile in Hawaii; Corazon Aquino sworn in as president

Index

Gordy Slack is a director of Free-Agents International, a news agency based in Oakland, California. He worked as a free-lance reporter in the Philippines during the final days of the Marcos regime and political ascension of Corazon Aquino in 1986. He has also worked as a staff reporter for the *Oakland Tribune* and *InfoWorld* magazine.

Arthur M. Schlesinger, jr., taught history at Harvard for many years and is currently Albert Schweitzer Professor of the Humanities at City University of New York. He is the author of numerous highly praised works in American history and has twice been awarded the Pulitzer Prize. He served in the White House as special assistant to Presidents Kennedy and Johnson.

PICTURE CREDITS

AP/Wide World Photos: pp. 14, 22, 29, 31, 34, 42, 46, 48, 51, 54, 58, 63, 65, 66, 68, 80, 82, 93, 97, 100; The Bettmann Archive: pp. 16, 17, 27, 28, 55; A. Hernandez/Sygma: p. 102; Reuters/Bettmann Newsphotos: pp. 12, 72, 88, 91, 94, 96, 98, 99, 101, 104, 106; Donna Sinisgalli: p. 15; Sygma: pp. 74, 79, 92; A. Tannenbaum/Sygma: p. 105; UPI/Bettmann Newsphotos: pp. 2, 17, 18, 19, 24, 32, 33, 36, 37, 38, 39, 40, 43, 44, 45, 47, 50, 52, 53, 56, 60, 62, 67, 69, 70, 71, 73, 76, 83, 85, 86, 90